MW01257751

TO:

FROM:

DATE:

THE

NEW

LONELINESS

DEVOTIONAL

CINDI McMENAMIN

HARVEST HOUSE PUBLISHERS
EUGENE, OREGON

Cover design by Bryce Williamson
Cover images © Victoria Gnatiuk / Getty Images
Interior design by Aesthetic Soup

For bulk, special sales, or ministry purchases, please call 1-800-547-8979.
Email: CustomerService@hhpbooks.com

The New Loneliness Devotional

Copyright © 2025 by Cindi McMenamin
Published by Harvest House Publishers
Eugene, Oregon 97408
www.harvesthousepublishers.com

ISBN 978-0-7369-8925-1 (hardcover)
ISBN 978-0-7369-8926-8 (eBook)

Library of Congress Control Number: 2024950191

Printed in China

25 26 27 28 29 30 31 32 33 / DC / 10 9 8 7 6 5 4 3 2 1

For Dana

You are a "city set on a hill" (Matthew 5:14),

and you bring light to all who know you.

Your dad and I are so grateful for your compassionate

heart and your industrious spirit.

Keep shining brightly for Him.

CONTENTS

Part II: Connecting with One Another

Part III: Connecting with Your Purpose

NO MORE LONELY DAYS

*L*ife can feel lonely.

Who do you really *know* anymore? And who *really* knows you? In this high-tech post-pandemic world, isolation is beginning to feel normal (if not inevitable) and many people spend more time with screens than humans. What started as a novelty became a necessity and now it's wreaking havoc on our health—mentally, emotionally, spiritually, and even physically.

You and I have, perhaps unknowingly, become a part of the epidemic of loneliness. The US Surgeon General issued a general advisory in mid-2023 calling loneliness, isolation, and lack of connection a public health crisis in this country. The report states there is an epidemic of loneliness, raising the onset of dementia by 50 percent and premature death by 60 percent.[1] Not having a sense of community and close connection with others is now one of the unhealthiest habits you can have—as dangerous as smoking up to 15 cigarettes a day! While aloneness is nothing new, the *new loneliness*—brought on by our increasing reliance on tech, combined with our post-COVID habits—is life-threatening.

An increase in abuse, addiction, anxiety, awareness of past wounds, and perceived failures has exacerbated the problem and made many of us feel even less sure of ourselves when it comes to developing authentic and transparent relationships with others. Even being among other people can make us feel different, awkward, alone.

What is making *you* feel lonely today? Are you single and wishing you had a man—or more friends—in your life? Are you overwhelmed with work and responsibilities at home and feeling you no longer have a social life? Are you trying to juggle it all and feeling as though you are failing? Are you starting to sink in despair because of a lack of hope and direction? Maybe you feel disappointed that you don't have what others have. Perhaps you are feeling stressed, overwhelmed, burdened, or anxious, and at times, you feel that no one else understands.

Regardless of what is making you feel unsupported, anxious, or disappointed, you don't have to feel lonely any longer. The God who fashioned you in your mother's womb and assigned the exact place and time that you'd live is the same One who goes before you, walks alongside you, and always has your back. He's also the One who is *with* you, *for* you, and has a very specific reason for why you are here. He's the One who promises to never leave, and to always be enough when you feel you need more. He's the One who whispers to you, "Because of your trust in My Son, you are *more* than enough. And you will never walk alone."

I encourage you to come daily to this book over the next 50 days to drink from the well of His Word and bask in the knowledge of His delight in you. Keep your Bible beside you and look up the passages I'm writing about, and read them in context to glean even more. Pray the prayers aloud at the end of each devotion and make them your own. And accept the daily challenge as a way of applying and embracing what you've read. As you take a few minutes each day to focus on God's Word and His ways, you'll discover a closer connection with the Lover of your soul. And you just may discover the ways He is nudging you to break out of the lonely shell you're in and experience community with others He brings your way.

You have no idea how much He's been waiting to get up close and personal with you, and convince you that you never truly walk alone. He's always, *always* there. And He's ready to pull you closer and show you what it means to commune with Him and others He has *already* brought into your life.

In Isaiah 30, God urged the Israelites to repent for forming an alliance with Egypt and looking everywhere else but to Him for their strength and provision. Through the prophet Isaiah's words, God expressed His patient, loving heart toward His people and confirmed to them that they would sense His presence and direction as long as they looked and listened for it. I believe these words can apply to us today as a tender reminder of His constant presence, refreshment, and direction if we listen for His voice:

> The Lord longs to be gracious to you, and therefore He waits on high to have compassion on you. For the Lord is a God of justice; How blessed are all those who long for Him…
>
> He will certainly be gracious to you at the sound of your cry; when He hears it, He will answer you…He…will no longer hide Himself, but your eyes will see your Teacher. Your ears will hear a word behind you, saying, "This is the way, walk in it," whenever you turn to the right or to the left (verses 18-21).

Just as God whispered His direction and a reminder of His presence to His people in the Old Testament, He will be there for you too. Let's not miss it.

Yours for a closer connection with Jesus, the Lover of your soul,

Cindi

PART I

CONNECTING WITH GOD'S HEART

WELCOMING THE QUIET

*Come with me by yourselves to a quiet place
and get some rest.*

MARK 6:31 NIV

*D*o you ever feel uncomfortable in the quiet, especially when you're alone?

While we may long for quiet in the midst of the constant chatter of televisions or podcasts, or the chaos of work or arguing children, what do we do with stillness, when there's no one else in the room and we start to feel alone?

Perhaps when it's quiet, our thoughts become louder—thoughts we don't want running through our minds. Or maybe the stillness makes us feel that no one is there to support us or understand what we're dealing with.

You and I can view quiet alone times as reminders of our loneliness and do everything we can to avoid them. Or, we can welcome them as much-needed respites from the noise—as invitations from God, who has been whispering to us, "Come with Me to a quiet place and get some rest."

When my husband left home for four days to climb another mountain with his friend, I realized the quiet times in the house afforded me something I had truly missed—the opportunity to spend more uninterrupted alone time with Jesus, the Lover of my soul. I relished being alone with Him and His Word on my back patio, alone with Him on a walking trail midday with no expectation from anyone of when I'd return. Alone with Him on the couch in the quiet of the evening, just me and my Lord.

> Oh, to be *weaned from my own life* and become fully dependent on the One who calls to me in the quiet!

Don't misunderstand. I *love* to be around people. I live for the lunch date or get-together with friends. And I enjoy having my husband home in the evenings when, for so many years, he was gone at work. But as I grow more in love with my Lord, I long for the alone times—more and more—to commune with Him. I long for the quiet to dwell on thoughts of Him and His loving thoughts toward me (Psalm 139:17).

How often we feel we must *set aside* time to be with God and then feel guilty for not doing it. How often our hearts may long for a getaway with Him, not realizing that getaway is available to us every moment of the day because He indwells us and calls us to come to Him within the recesses of our hearts.

"Be still, and *know* that I am God," says Psalm 46:10 (NIV). We can get to know Him in the stillness as we allow Him to quiet our thoughts and we focus on His presence.

Psalm 46:10 in the New American Standard Bible reads, "*Stop striving* and know that I am God." Having a heart at rest means we are not striving to control, not anxious nor stressed about what might happen or all that we have to do. It means we are in a place of quiet contentment like David sang in Psalm 131:2: "I have calmed and quieted my soul, like a weaned child with its mother; like a weaned child is my soul within me" (ESV).

Quiet. Full. Satisfied. Secure.

In another version, that verse reads: "I have quieted myself and caused my soul to become silent, that I might be as a child that is weaned of his mother, as one who is weaned from my own life" (JUB).

Oh, to be *weaned from my own life* and become fully dependent on the One who calls to me in the quiet!

Is it time to slow your pace, switch off the inner chatter, and ask God to still your mind from anxiety or busyness and flood it with His peace? Is it time to close the app, shut the lid on your device, or turn off the music or the TV, and develop a heart that not only welcomes but longs for the quiet stillness? It's there you will begin to discern your Savior's voice, which is much more loving than your own internal critic. It is there you will hear His tender words: "I have loved you with an everlasting love...I have drawn you out with kindness" (Jeremiah 31:3). It is there you will be assured of His promise to never leave you nor abandon you (Hebrews 13:5). It is there, in *His* presence, that you will find fullness of joy (Psalm 16:11).

Lord Jesus, I want to spend more focused time with You, the Lover of my soul. Help me to welcome the quiet times in my life and see them not as reminders of loneliness but as invitations to be alone with You. You are the One who pursues my heart. Calm my ambitions and my striving and help me to be like a child, content to lean against You in the quiet, and just rest.

TODAY'S CHALLENGE

Embrace the quiet of your day—or escape to it by carving it out some-where—so you can get away with God in your heart. Close your eyes. Enjoy the stillness of the moment and the assurance of His presence. Spend some time thanking Him for breathing rest—and quiet—into your day.

IN HIS IMAGE

God created man in His own image,
in the image of God He created him;
male and female He created them.

GENESIS 1:27

ave you noticed the trend? We often refer to ourselves—
and our daily activities—in electronic terms as if we
were devices. In our culture, as well as across the world,
many people use *Google* as a verb and often feel more comfortable with
their electronic devices than with one another. I can't help but think this
makes us feel more alone than ever—like objects rather than people, and
digital codes rather than designed creations.

We are often encouraged to *plug into* a church and to *unplug* from our
busyness. After a conference or webinar, we want to *defrag* from information overload. When we're high on adrenaline, we consider ourselves
wired; when we're burnt out, we say we've *run down the battery.* When
we need to rest, we say we must *recharge.*

And our interpersonal relationships are now *internet* relationships.
Face time used to mean what it sounds like, and it didn't involve a phone,

tablet, or laptop screen. *Social* used to mean *talking* or *being* with one another, not scrolling on a device.

"Can we Zoom about this later? I don't have the bandwidth for it right now."

You and I were made in the image of God, not in the likeness of a smartphone. Our sustainer is God Almighty, not Apple, Microsoft, Google, or Amazon!

So how do we reclaim (or just remind ourselves of) our human status as God's creation, made in His image and for His glory? We can start by rethinking how we speak about and define ourselves.

Next time you are drained of power and need to recharge (your body *or* your phone), let your device run dry and keep it off for (gasp!) an hour or two. If you fall behind with what happened on social media, your notifications will likely let you know. And if you miss a call, someone can leave a message (all phones have voicemail, like those old-fashioned desktop answering machines back in the day when you—or your parents—had far more time and space in your day for creativity, meaningful conversations, and thoughtful execution of what you deemed your top priority).

God never told us in His Word to hurry up, produce more, or run down the battery. His words resonate at a different pace: "Be still, and know that I am God" (Psalm 46:10 ESV); and "Come to Me, all who are weary and burdened, and I will give you rest" (Matthew 11:28). Yet our next-day or even "same-day delivery with Prime" has made us even more incapable of waiting on God who is not bound by time or delivery schedules. The words of the psalmists were not "Hurry up, God, I need an answer within the hour," but rather, "I wait for the Lord more than watchmen wait for the morning" (Psalm 130:6 NIV). Good things, rich things, priceless things come to those who wait on God and His perfect timing.

Do you need to revisit some of the things humans, rather than devices, do so you can become a vintage believer who experiences the beauty of waiting on God?

One of my favorite *humanizing* activities is my daily walk around a small lake near my home. I can't help but recognize and adore God when I'm outside among the beauty of His creation—away from technology, mobile devices, and anything with a screen or signal. It is then that I can tune in to *His* signals—a gentle breeze, the way He parts the clouds and sends the sun's rays to shine through, the song of a bird, the rustle of leaves, and the reminder that "the earth is the LORD's and the fullness thereof" (Psalm 24:1 ESV). As you slow down and get outside and off your phone, you may rediscover the beauty of your Creator (not your Programmer) who calls you His masterpiece (Ephesians 2:10 NLT).

According to the Westminster Catechism, man's chief end is to glorify God, and to enjoy Him forever. That means we were created to worship. (Do I dare say we are *wired* for it?) Being out in the beauty of His creation and worshipping Him reminds me of the Luke 19 account when Jesus rode triumphantly into Jerusalem on a young colt and the Pharisees demanded He rebuke His followers for waving their palm branches and crying out praise to Him, their king. Jesus told the Pharisees if the people remained silent, "the very stones would cry out" (verse 40 ESV).

He *must* be praised. And we are the ones *created* to do it.

Don't leave your God-given calling and purpose to the rocks! Get off your device, notice God and the people all around you, and give Him, not your phone, the attention He deserves.

Lord, what if zeal for Your Word, not the contents of my phone, were to consume me? Help my worship time to exceed my screen time so I am reminded of who I am in Your eyes.

TODAY'S CHALLENGE

Turn off your phone for half an hour (or leave it at home) and go outside to enjoy the presence of God and a break from tech. This may be what reinvigorates your soul so you can once again hear God's voice.

AS CLOSE AS YOUR BREATH

The LORD is near to the brokenhearted
and saves those who are crushed in spirit.

PSALM 34:18

D o you sometimes feel like God is far away?

Heartbreak, struggles, hurts from the past, unanswered prayers, or filling your schedule with everything but Him can make you believe God is distant. But Scripture abounds with evidence that He is as close to you as the air you breathe.

Psalm 139 assures us that God knows every detail of our lives, and in verses 7-12, we read there's nowhere we can go to get outside of His presence and away from His watchful eye. Hebrews 13:5 also tells us He will never leave us nor forsake us. But maybe you know all that and you still long to know He's there.

When we feel like God is far away, it's often because we are the ones who have distanced ourselves. Perhaps other loves have stolen our heart. The feeling that He's distant can be an indicator that we need to put ourselves in the position where we can sense His presence, hear His voice, notice His work around us, and invite Him closer to our hearts.

Tiffany, a young married professional, told me, "There have definitely been moments in my life when I felt God was far away, but looking back, I was hesitant to truly bring my struggles before Him. I know now that if I fully pour my heart out to Him, I will feel that He is with me in that moment."

How can you be assured God is right next to you?

Take a Divine Pause—Sometimes we can't sense God's presence because there's too much of everything else going on. Too much noise. Too much confusion. Too much anxiety. Too many apps or windows open. Too many voices and thoughts running through our minds. Center your mind on Him (Colossians 3:1-2) and start to breathe deeply. Try it. Exhale the distracting thoughts. Inhale a desire to sense His presence. Exhale your preoccupation with self. Inhale a desire to know Him more completely. Exhale the worries of the moment. Inhale His peace. Now, don't you feel closer to His heart already? There's a reason His Word says, "Be *still*, and know that I am God" (Psalm 46:10 ESV).

Whisper His Name—There are times we need God but we just don't know what to say or where to begin. Start by saying His name and then speak your heart's cry. Scripture says there is power in the name of Jesus, not only because "salvation is found in no one else, for there is no other name under heaven given to men by which we must be saved" (Acts 4:12 NIV), but because Jesus responds to His name when His loved ones call to Him.

The writers of the classics called this type of whispering cry "breath prayers." My breath prayers to sense His presence are "Jesus, I need You," or "Jesus, give me a heart for You." Calling upon His name is one of the simplest ways to sense His presence. And I believe the simplest of cries are the ones that penetrate His heart—and ours—the quickest.

Read His Word Aloud—God speaks to us through His Word. And one of the best ways to sense His presence is to get into His Word and ask His Holy Spirit to guide you into a better understanding of it. When you read God's Word, and even speak it audibly, you will sense its power and His presence. The Bible says God's Word is "living and active, and sharper than any two-edged sword" (Hebrews 4:12). That sharp sword will prick your heart through conviction, inspiration, enlightenment, or determination. A pricked heart is better than a numb, dull, or complacent heart any day, so get into His Word and find Him there.

> "If your heart is broken, you'll find God right there; if you're kicked in the gut, he'll help you catch your breath."

Start Praising Him—God inhabits the praises of His people. Ever wondered why you sometimes feel closer to God when you're in a church service, singing hymns or praise songs? It's possibly because that's where worship tends to take place. But you don't have to be in a church building among other believers in order to worship Him. Worship is praise and acknowledgment of His worthiness wherever you are and in whatever situation you are in. Worship is surrender. Worship is giving Him your time, talents, and treasure.

When you start praising God regardless of where you are, you'll sense His presence, probably because you're no longer focused on yourself, but on Him. When you open the door of your heart to love Him, He will meet you there. Every time. In fact, Psalm 34:18 in *The Message* assures us God is always just a breath away…or just as close as our own breath:

> If your heart is broken, you'll find God right there;
> If you're kicked in the gut, he'll help you catch your breath.

Lord, thank You for never hiding from me. Your Word says I will find You when I search for You with all my heart (Jeremiah 29:13). Make Your presence known as close and real as the air I breathe.

TODAY'S CHALLENGE

Practice spiritual breathing by exhaling (breathing out your doubts), and inhaling (breathing in an expectation of God's presence). Breathe out your insistence on your own way; breathe in your desire for God's control.

HIS CALMING PRESENCE

Don't worry about anything; instead,
pray about everything.

PHILIPPIANS 4:6 NLT

*I*t's been said we are living in the most anxious times on Earth. Post-pandemic loneliness and a sense of isolation still impact many people, young and old alike. Suicide is at an all-time high, now the second-leading cause of death for children ages 10-14 and adults ages 20-34.[2] Countless people suffer from depression and anxiety disorders. Mental and emotional health issues are off the charts. Stress is making us more susceptible to cancer and other diseases.[3] Many struggle with a sense of identity, or lack of it. Financially, people are finding it difficult to make ends meet. And the US Surgeon General has declared loneliness a public health crisis and full-on epidemic with devastating results.

Where is God in all of this?

If you're like most believers today, you'll say you know in your mind that God is in control, but you have a hard time relying on Him in your day-to-day life. And what I've observed after decades of ministry is that those who can't bring that truth from their head to their heart—from the pages of God's Word to their daily life—also admit they need to be in the Word of God more and know it better.

To know God is to know His Word. To know His Word is to know Him. I once heard my mentor author, Elisabeth Elliot, say, "Pray with an open Bible. How can we know what to pray if we aren't reading God's Word? And how can we understand God's Word if we aren't praying?" The more you open up His Word (whether it's in book form or via an app on your device), the more He will open your eyes and heart to know who He is and how He can calm your anxious heart.

Philippians 4:6-7 has been a lifeline for me through the years—especially because there is much to worry about:

> when you're contemplating decisions that will impact your future
>
> when you're seeking a man to marry—or struggling in your marriage
>
> when you're pregnant—or trying to get pregnant
>
> when you're caring for a child, parent, or grandparent
>
> when you're trying to stay afloat financially
>
> when your health—or the health of someone you love—causes fear or frustration

Life is often accompanied by concerns that quickly turn into worries that can develop into fear or anxiety. Yet God's Word gives us a simple yet practical antidote to the type of worry that breeds fear. Philippians 4:6-7 instructs: "Don't worry about anything; instead, pray about everything. Tell God what you need, and thank him for all he has done. Then you will experience God's peace, which exceeds anything we can understand. His peace will guard your hearts and minds as you live in Christ Jesus" (NLT).

The next verse tells us what exactly to focus on. Our worries over what hasn't yet happened? The things we are anxious to control? The worst possible scenarios? *No.* "Fix your thoughts on what is true, and honorable, and right, and pure, and lovely, and admirable. Think about things that are excellent and worthy of praise" (verse 8 NLT). We are to focus on what is true—or *real*, not on what we *fear* will happen. We are to focus on what is "pure, and lovely, and admirable." Those descriptions sound like *God's characteristics*, not *our circumstances.* As we focus on the here and now, the true and real, and *all that God is*, "then the God of peace will be with you" (verse 9 NLT).

Do you really believe that? As you focus on what is true and real and all that is good about God and what He does for His children, peace will replace your worry. I can honestly tell you that every time I pray for something that bothers me or has the potential to, that concern never develops into fear, but instantly dissolves, as I realize God has heard me and He has taken that worrisome burden from me and replaced it with His indescribable peace.

He will do that for you too. You have only to ask.

Are you wishing you were closer to God than you are right now? Do you long to feel less anxious and more at peace as you trust this capable God with your concerns? Then start now. Open your Bible to Philippians 4:6-9. Pray through the verses (which means reading the words aloud to God as a prayer, inserting your name and situation into the passage), and He will answer. This is a promise. It is a guarantee. And it is your route to rest, freedom, and peace.

Lord, help me not to worry about anything, but to instead pray about everything. You know exactly what I need, and I thank You for working through this situation on my behalf. I trust Your promise to give me indescribable peace as I lay my concerns at Your feet and focus on what is real, pure, and admirable, like You.

TODAY'S CHALLENGE

The moment worry starts to creep into your mind, give it immediately to God in prayer and thank Him for what He's already doing about it. Then relax and experience His peace.

IN THE PALM OF HIS HAND

You have encircled me behind and in front,
and placed Your hand upon me.

PSALM 139:5

*I*t's easy to feel right now that the world is spinning out of control. Disease runs rampant. The economy is struggling. Our fears and anxieties mount. Political tensions are rising. Our national and religious freedoms are declining. Yet our God has everything under control. He has the world—and all who are in it—in the palm of His hand.

Haylee, an artist, wife, and mom of two young children, said, "Seeing so much suffering and chaos in the world has made me ask God a lot of questions. Not knowing why God allows the things He allows is what is most difficult, at times—be it sickness, evil rulers, and other matters. I just wonder why a lot."

As overwhelmed as Haylee is when she has too much on her to-do list, or when she wonders why things happen the way they do, still, she says, "I know God sees me and loves me, and His peace is the very thing that helps calm me down in times of stress."

Haylee finds comfort in God's Word and in worship music that she listens to or writes and composes herself to help her stay connected to His heart.

Psalm 139, a portion of worship music within the Word of God, tells us how intimately acquainted God is with all our ways. I can't help but think God included this song of David's in His inspired Word to help us connect with His heart, especially at times when we feel insignificant or helpless in light of all that is going on in the world. Not only does this song tell us God has searched us and known us and that He knows our every thought and every detail of our wandering, but it also says He protects us and loves us more than we know. Even when we feel like the world is spinning out of control.

"You hem me in, behind and before, and lay your hand upon me," David sang in verse 5 (ESV).

There is such peace in knowing God is here with us in the dark, in the light, waking up, falling asleep, going out, and coming in. In times of peace and in times of chaos, confusion, or unanswered questions. If you're one to get a little more anxious or stressed when watching or listening to the news, or scrolling through the happenings in this country or around the world, keep your eyes on God's Word, which constantly reassures us Who is ultimately in control.

Psalm 139 reminds us that we never need to worry about anything concerning our life or the lives of those we love because of God's ever-present watchfulness. From this song alone, we are assured that God is One who

- searches us and knows us from the inside out (verse 1)

- knows our every thought and action (verses 2-3)

- knows what we will say before we say it (verse 4)

- encircles us and places His hand of protection upon us (verse 5)

- follows us everywhere we go—or stays with us when we can't go anywhere (verses 8-12)

- formed us and watched over us while we were in the womb (verses 13-15)

- wrote out our life story in His book before we lived it— meaning even this time of your questioning doesn't take Him by surprise (verse 16)

- thinks innumerable (and precious) thoughts of us (verses 17-18)

- knows our concerns and anxieties—including during uncertain days like these (verse 23)

- convicts us of our offenses and leads us in the right direction (verse 24)

This psalm reassures us that God is intimately acquainted with us *and* our loved ones. And He is aware of what is going on in the hearts and lives of those we can't be with on a daily basis. It assures us there is nothing we can do and no place we can go where God's love doesn't follow. That means there is never a reason to worry or feel alone. I am safe—and *you* are safe—in the palm of His hand.

God knows every detail of the paths we walk, the decisions we make, the words we say, and the actions we carry out. He knows every detail about us and the world we live in. And He will never let us out of His sight or out of His heart. He tracks us better than our phones; His knowledge surpasses Siri and Google; He always has our best in mind. You may be one who never goes anywhere without your phone. But you are certainly one who never goes anywhere without His watchful, loving eye and His tender, compassionate hand.

Lord, thank You that You know the condition of this world and the condition of my heart. Thank You that Your love follows me everywhere I go, and that I am safe and secure in the palm of Your protective, loving hand.

TODAY'S CHALLENGE

Each time you hear discouraging or disturbing news about this world—or your personal circumstances—whisper the words, "This did not take God by surprise." Saying this will remind you that He is still on the throne.

NOWHERE ELSE TO GO

Jesus said to the twelve, "You do not want to leave also, do you?" Simon Peter answered Him, "Lord, to whom shall we go? You have words of eternal life."

John 6:67-68

I remember the moment in which I truly felt I had nowhere else to go but to God. My parents had just split up and there was no security in my home, my plans, or my heart. Today I look back on that day as the moment in which I took ownership of my faith.

When you grow up learning about Jesus from the time you're young, or if you've walked with Him for a while, you can get complacent and put your life on cruise control and fail to acknowledge His presence, direction, wisdom, guidance, and love every moment of your day. Faith can easily become a compartment that is added to the many elements of your life instead of becoming your *whole* life.

The apostle Paul opened chapter 3 of his letter to the Colossians with instructions for followers if they are truly His:

> Therefore, *if* you have been raised with Christ, keep seek-
> ing the things that are above, where Christ is, seated at
> the right hand of God. Set your minds on the things that
> are above, not on the things that are on earth. For
> you have died, and your life is hidden with Christ in
> God. When Christ, *who is our life*, is revealed, then you
> also will be revealed with Him in glory (verses 1-4).

If you have been raised with Christ. This appears to be an if/then situation. *If* we are His, and we have truly been transformed by His death
and resurrection (2 Corinthians 5:17), we are to keep seeking the things
that are above, where Christ is. That means we are to keep our minds on
our eternal home, have eternal priorities and values, and live as if we are
here temporarily and we will soon be in our real home with the Lover of
our soul. The passage goes on to say we have died, and our lives are hidden with Christ in God. (Our lives, our rights, our sense of entitlement,
our preferences have died with Christ, and we [our original natures] are
hidden and He [and His character—Galatians 5:22-23] is evident and
on display for the world to see.) Then the next line in the passage simply assumes that Christ is not merely a part of our life, but *is our life*.

When we consider Him—not a boyfriend, husband, child, or even
a job—as our whole life, we safeguard ourselves from misplaced priorities and frequent disappointment.

People will always disappoint us. But Jesus never will.

A friend once told me to lower my expectations of others, or I would
always be disappointed. While that advice seemed callous at the time,
today I know it to be true. Others mean well, but they will always disappoint us in one way or another. Only when our expectations are with

the Lord will we find He is fully reliable. And if we feel disappointed in God, we are apparently believing something about Him that isn't true.

God is the only one who will never disappoint us. I know you've heard that too. And like me, you believe it in your heart of hearts, but life still hurts. Being vulnerable enough to tell a loved one what you need from them and then coming up empty because they have no idea how to respond can leave you feeling sore to the core.

So where do you and I go with that? Our answer must be the same as Peter's: "Lord, there is no one else that we can go to!" (John 6:68 CEV).

I have learned to echo Peter's words by making Psalm 73:25-26 my life's motto, as well as the cry of my heart:

> Whom have I in heaven but you? And there is nothing on earth that I desire besides you. My flesh and my heart may fail, but God is the strength of my heart and my portion forever (ESV).

In the Contemporary English Version, those two verses read:

> In heaven I have only you,
> and on this earth
> you are all I want.
> My body and mind may fail,
> but you are my strength
> and my choice forever.

In other words, *Christ, who is my life.*

Where do *you* go when others disappoint? Be already depending on Him, and the disappointments will come less often. What do you do when you begin to lack contentment? Remember who is your life and that in His presence is fullness of joy (Psalm 16:11). Where do you turn when you feel directionless or lacking in purpose? To the One who is your life, your compass, your purpose.

Lord, may You be the object of my heart, my focus, my direction, my life. You gave up Your life so I could belong to You forever. I give You my life and desires and realize I have nowhere else to go—but to You.

TODAY'S CHALLENGE

Say aloud "Jesus is the only one who will never disappoint" as a way of cementing that truth in your heart. The more your expectations are in Him alone, the less you will be disappointed.

HIS UNWAVERING LOVE

*When he was still a long way off, his father
saw him and felt compassion for him,
and ran and embraced him and kissed him.*

Luke 15:20

I will always be moved by the story of the lost son who returned to his father. The son's repentance and return isn't what impacts me the most, but the loving father's response.

We call it the story of the prodigal son. The word *prodigal* literally means one who spends money in a reckless, extravagant way. This younger son asked his father for his inheritance early. (In Jewish custom, that would be the equivalent of saying, "I wish you were dead.") He then took his share of what was still legally his father's, went to a faraway land, and squandered his entire inheritance on foolish, reckless, raunchy living. He was living high on the hog, rich with money and "friends," until he found himself sleeping with the pigs, penniless and alone. Starving, and upon realizing he was envying the pigs for the slop they got to eat, he decided to return home and ask if he could be his father's hired hand.

Then at least he would be fed better than pigs and have a place to sleep among his father's servants.

The journey home must have been long and grueling for this man who, by this time, was smelly, scrawny, and had been homeless for quite some time. He was without food, water, proper clothing, or even good shoes, which only increased his shame and humiliation. Perhaps he had a speech prepared, an admission of his wrongdoing, a pleading for his father to consider taking him in as a servant. Or maybe he intended to fall in shame at his father's feet and beg to be heard. But before he could utter a word, his father surprised, shocked, and overwhelmed him with a greeting he did not expect to receive.

His father's pride was at stake with the return of a son whom he should consider dead to him. How he reacted would set an example to other Jewish families when their rebellious sons acted with such disrespect and contempt. This father, upon seeing *from a distance* that the scraggly man making his way up the road was not some homeless derelict or demon-possessed wanderer, but his long-lost son, picked up the ends of his robe and *ran* to meet him. Before the shamed son could utter a word to express the humiliation on his heart, his father embraced him, held onto him like there was no tomorrow, and ordered his servants to give his son a robe (representing his position as a son) and a ring (indicating his authority once again as an estate holder). The father then ordered that plans be made to celebrate the homecoming of his wayward son. He threw a party!

This son, who was once thought dead, was now alive. He had returned home. There was no punishment. No lecture, no shaming, no rebuke, and no harsh words. Just grace. Forgiveness. Abundant love.

I used to think this story was a warning to not rebel—that it was about the consequences of disobedience and the importance of repentance. But the story isn't so much about the rebellious child, but about the patient, persevering, forgiving father—the one who wouldn't think for a second to relegate his child from heir to servant. His child's position in the family didn't change as a result of disrespectful actions or heinous circumstances. Only the son's heart had changed—and become calloused—toward his father. His father's love for him, however, had never wavered.

Do you realize, precious sister in Christ, that no matter what you and I do, we can't undo God's love for us? We can't position ourselves out of our inheritance in Christ. We can't disappoint Him to the point that He cancels us or unfriends us or relegates us to "outside-the-house" status and lets us visit once or twice a year at Easter or Christmas. The door to His home is always open. In fact, once we've been allowed in to dwell with Him, it never closes to us. *Our* door is the one we shut—the door to our hearts that causes Him to stand and knock and ask to come in (Revelation 3:20).

> Do you realize, precious sister in Christ, that no matter what you and I do, we can't undo God's love for us?

Won't you open the door of your heart to this Compassionate Father or return to Him and dwell with Him continually? His invitation to you has never expired; His patience has never worn thin; His love has never run dry. Run to *Him* and experience His loving embrace.

Lord Jesus, You have never allowed me to be a stranger to You; may You never be a neglected guest in my heart and home. Thank You for being the Father to whom I can run, ever trust, always love.

TODAY'S CHALLENGE

In what way do you need to return to the love and embrace of your Heavenly Father? Talk to Him about it now. He's waiting for—no, He's *running* toward—you.

THE ROOT OF YOUR FEARS

There is no fear in love, but perfect love drives out fear,
because fear involves punishment, and the
one who fears is not perfected in love.

1 JOHN 4:18

o you fear God won't come through for you because of something you've done or failed to do? Perhaps you are fearing the worst will happen in your circumstances when you really don't have a reason for such fears.

None of us are strangers to fear. Our fears range from living out our lives alone, to not being able to make a difference in this world, to losing someone or something precious to us. Often, our fears are rooted in a misunderstanding of who God really is. We can tend to see Him as one who is angry and has no intention of letting us enjoy our lives. Or we may think God is keeping a tally of our good versus bad actions, intending to pay us back for mistakes we've made in the past. Perhaps you believe God will think long and hard before coming to your rescue when you find you are in need.

But God isn't an angry God eager to strike back at you with a vengeance. He isn't looking at a checklist, waiting to see when you'll earn or deserve His favor. He isn't stingy when it comes to His mercy and His kindness. Throughout Psalm 136, we are told His "faithfulness is everlasting" and in the ESV, that song repeatedly tells us God's "steadfast love endures forever." He is a God whose mercy never ends and who *loves* to care for His children.

Jesus said if we, being human and sinful, know how to give good gifts to our children, how much more will our Father who is in heaven give good things to those who ask Him? (Matthew 7:11).

He's also a God who wants you to love and trust Him as a child would trust a loving, dependable parent. Hebrews 11:6 says, "Without faith it is impossible to please Him, for the one who comes to God must believe that He exists, and that He proves to be One who rewards those who seek Him."

God wants your faith—not your fear—that He really *can* come through for you. But to have faith in Him, you must know who He is and be convinced He's trustworthy.

The Bible tells us there is no fear in love, but perfect love *drives out* fear (1 John 4:18). That means if you love God perfectly, you will trust Him completely, and where there is complete trust, there is no room for fear.

How can you increase your trust in God and know without a doubt that He'll come through for you?

Let go of the guilt that causes you to fear God's punishment. We all have baggage that we, by nature, try to hide. But God wants to release you of the guilt and shame in your past. Psalm 32:5 says, "I acknowledged my sin to You, and my iniquity I did not hide; I said, 'I will confess my transgressions to the LORD'; and You forgave the guilt of my sin." Not only does God forgive us of our past wrongs when we are truly sorry for them, He removes them from our record—as far as the east is from the west (Psalm 103:12). Confess your sin and believe He's forgiven you.

Look to Scripture to reshape your understanding of God. Regardless of what you may perceive about God, Scripture says He has loved you with an everlasting love (Jeremiah 31:3); He laid down His life to suffer *in your place* so you would not have to be separated from Him for eternity (Romans 5:8); and "nothing can ever separate us from God's love" (Romans 8:38 NLT). Death can't, and life can't. The angels can't, and the demons can't. Your fears for today, your worries about tomorrow, and even the powers of hell can't keep God's love away from you when put your trust in Christ Jesus.

> Your fears for today, your worries about tomorrow, and even the powers of hell can't keep God's love away from you when put your trust in Christ Jesus.

Let God show you His softer side. It wasn't until I started *looking* for God's softer side that I saw Him as my Protector, Provider, Rescuer, Daddy, Loving Husband, Friend, and so much more. Everything I have needed—*and* wanted—He is. In Jeremiah 29:13, God said, "You will seek Me *and find Me* when you search for Me with all your heart." Look for the God who pursues your heart. And let His perfect love drive out your fear.

Lord, thank You for being a good, loving, dependable Father who always has my back. You deserve my complete trust. Help me to believe You will come through for me in whatever I need today— and always.

TODAY'S CHALLENGE

Tell God exactly what you're frightened of—or write it out in the space below—as a way of handing it to Him. He already knows your fear, but by telling Him, you are placing it in His capable hands and recognizing it's something He no longer wants you to carry—or worry about.

WHEN UNCERTAINTY LOOMS

Let all that I am wait quietly before God,
for my hope is in him.
He alone is my rock and my salvation,
my fortress where I will not be shaken.

PSALM 62:5-6 NLT

Could anything seem longer than waiting for the results of a biopsy?

Blessed with great health and only one hospitalization in my lifetime (which was my daughter's birth via C-section), I believed I was in the category of people who might never have to endure a cancer scare—or a cancer reality.

Until the evening my sister noticed what looked like a ping-pong ball protruding from my neck. I had just finished taking an antibiotic for a sinus infection (my first one in decades!) that had sidelined me for about nine days. "That's just swollen lymph nodes," I told my sister. "My body's been fighting an infection." But Kristi persisted: "Please see a doctor. I *know* you…your neck shouldn't look like that."

I was able to see a doctor three days later, had blood drawn that same afternoon, and through what must have been a miracle, was able to schedule an ultrasound for that same evening. By the next morning, I was able to read my ultrasound report online: a five-centimeter nodule on my right thyroid lobe—"high-risk category." I then joined the ranks of those who know what it's like to wait *two long weeks* for a call from a doctor that might turn my world around.

While the natural reaction to uncertainty is to worry, or to google our symptoms to try to learn more, or to talk to others who can share their stories and calculate our odds, the *supernatural* God-empowered response is to take it to the One who knows it all, sees it all, and can heal it all. He's even been known to eliminate it all. When He is our all in all, there is nothing at all that can move us or shake us.

Nothing touches you or me that hasn't first passed through God's loving hands. He is capable. He knows what He's doing. We can rest.

David's prayer in Psalm 62:5-6 comforted my heart and became my own:

> Let all that I am wait quietly before God,
>> for my hope is in him.
> He alone is my rock and my salvation,
>> my fortress where I will not be shaken (NLT).

As soon as I prayed that verse aloud, God's peace flooded my soul. Whether or not I had cancer wasn't my overriding concern anymore. The only thing that mattered to me in that moment was that God be pleased with my response—now and through whatever lay ahead.

I wanted to respond to my uncertain future as God's faithful ones had before me.

- Like Job, who said, "Though He slay me, I will hope in Him" (Job 13:15).

- Like David, who said in Psalm 23:4, "Though I walk through the valley of the shadow of death, I fear no evil, for You are with me; Your rod and Your staff, they comfort me."

- Like David, again, who said, "Though I walk in the midst of trouble, You will revive me" (Psalm 138:7).

- And like the prophet Habukkuk, who said, "Though the fig trees have no blossoms, and there are no grapes on the vines…even though the flocks die in the fields, and the cattle barns are empty, yet I will rejoice in the Lord! I will be joyful in the God of my salvation!" (3:17-18 NLT).

Those statements from Scripture's men of faith became my declarations: *Though* He slay me…*Though* I walk through the valley of the shadow of death…*Though* the fig tree should not blossom…*Though* this may happen, I will still trust. Those were my variables, my circumstances. *If* this happens, God, I'll still trust. But alongside my *thoughs* and *ifs*, God had His *whens*…His promises for *when*—not *if*—I go through situations that appear threatening.

- "*When* my spirit felt weak within me, You knew my path" (Psalm 142:3).

- "*When* you walk, your steps will not be hampered; and if you run, you will not stumble" (Proverbs 4:12).

- "*When* you pass through the waters, I will be with you; and through the rivers, they will not overflow you. *When* you walk through the fire, you will not be scorched, nor will the flame burn you" (Isaiah 43:2).

Will you trust God with whatever comes your way today, knowing nothing takes Him by surprise? Will you trust that what feels like awful timing is all part of His perfect schedule? Will you share your heart and concern with a sister in Christ who will pray for you and with you and walk you through this, whether it's rejoicing with you over what God averted or holding your hand through what He is allowing you to endure?

Lord God, I wait quietly before You, knowing You alone are my fortress and I will not be shaken.

TODAY'S CHALLENGE

What worry or concern do you need to surrender to God today? In a journal or in the space below, write it out as a prayer of surrender. He's already walked through it ahead of you and He's capable of carrying you through it if and when it's time.

WRAPPED IN HIS LOVE

*My frame was not hidden from You
when I was made in secret.*

Psalm 139:15

I still remember the haunting words of my friend Edie as I sat across the table from her at lunch 20 years ago.

"When I was first diagnosed with cancer, I couldn't shake the feeling that God didn't love me anymore," she said.

Her touching story told me that as close as we may feel to God, when disappointment comes or disaster strikes, we can begin to wonder if He still has us in His hand of protection, if He still cares, if He still loves us.

"I didn't feel He was punishing me," she said. "A lot of people get cancer. But I did feel that He couldn't possibly love me anymore." Through her cancer ordeal, Edie grew closer to the Lord, and she gained a powerful testimony as a cancer survivor many times over. Yet she lived fully alive, full of joy and peace, and into her seventies fully knowing throughout most of her life—and especially at the time of her death—that her Savior had never stopped loving her.

Through the years, I have often asked God to never let me feel that He no longer loves me if and when the day comes that I learn I have cancer.

The day I received my ultrasound results of a high-risk mass on my right thyroid lobe, I felt covered in a blanket of His love. I can't explain this, but instead of fear or feeling unloved, neglected, or discriminated against, I felt so very loved and tenderly set apart for whatever God had in store. It wasn't until a few days later, as I was telling my sister about God's loving embrace through it all, that I remembered that conversation with Edie more than two decades earlier, and my resulting prayers that God would never let me feel He had abandoned me.

All this time, I believed my greatest fear was getting cancer, but God knew—and remembered—my greatest fear was that He would no longer love me.

Our God knows what each of us needs and He is providing it. Yet we need to pay attention and listen for His loving voice, not those destructive thoughts that seek to debilitate us when bad news comes our way.

A biopsy of the lump showed it wasn't cancerous, but it was "atypical," so I opted to have it monitored for size every four to six months instead of having it surgically removed, due to the risks that kind of surgery would pose to my vocal chords. I remember feeling such peace that God would shrink or eliminate the mass and that this was my test of faith to believe He really could heal as a result of prayer. Yet four months later, an ultrasound did not show a decrease in the size of the mass. Rather, the mass had grown substantially and had begun acting like an aggressive form of thyroid cancer.

God, why did You make it clear I was to wait and monitor this lump when You knew it would keep growing and eventually need to come out?

Why did You not eliminate it or at least shrink it while I waited and prayed? Why did You allow it to get bigger and possibly further complicate the risks to my voice if I have it removed?

I felt discouraged—until I could quiet the voices in my mind to make room for His.

I want to keep you here a little longer because you and I have never been closer, He seemed to whisper to my heart.

God knew, during this time of uncertainty, that I had never prayed to Him more intensely, communed with Him more often, and depended on Him more fully. And apparently, He didn't want to let go of that quite yet.

Sometimes unanswered prayers aren't so much about what we are praying for (like healing or the elimination of our problem), but more about God wanting to pull us closer to His heart and show us what faith and trust really look like. Was my faith in what He would *do*? Or was my faith simply in Him and *whatever* He decided to do?

Through a scheduling miracle, I was able to have the mass surgically removed just before the end of that year. And through God's provision and grace, there was no negative impact on my voice. God carried me through that surgery as He had intended to do all along. And I can honestly tell you I know Him better today than I did before that lump was discovered.

God knows what runs through our blood, what lurks in our tissues and glands, and what tumors might be present in our bodies that doctors haven't yet discovered. Our very existence depends on His grace, and when you and I get a health scare, we can lean in to His heavenly embrace and trust that He knows what He's allowing, and that His ways are always better than ours (Isaiah 55:8-11).

Lord, thank You for wrapping me in Your love and caring so much about my relationship with You.

TODAY'S CHALLENGE

Is there any circumstance that would make you question God's love for you? If so, bring it to God today. He knows the fears you need to surrender.

SECURE IN HIM

My sheep listen to My voice, and I know them...
and no one will snatch them out of My hand.

JOHN 10:27-28

I remember being confused the day I was told to pray for a mom at my daughter's school when she had her identity stolen.

What? How ridiculous! I remember thinking. *How can someone steal from us who we are?*

Yes, that was before the term *identity theft* was a household phrase, and before the phenomenon had impacted nearly every person who has a credit card or has ever shopped online.

It wasn't long thereafter that my husband and I experienced our own version of identity theft when we discovered online purchases from our checking account that we didn't make. It turned out that orders paid by our credit cards were being delivered to someone who lived across the street. (Someone had been going through our trash, collecting bills and receipts I'd thrown out because it hadn't occurred to me to have them shredded due to creeps like him!)

That's when I understood our identity was no longer defined by our personalities and uniqueness, but our numbers—our driver's license numbers, social security numbers, credit card and bank numbers, phone numbers, mailing addresses, and birthdates. If someone has all or even some of that data, they can build a profile of you and make other people think they *are* you when shopping online with your information, and even when emailing your friends or sending someone private messages, or "chatting" with them from a fake or hacked social media account of yours.

Yet shouldn't that be called identity *copying*, or identity *fabrication*? But…identity *theft*? How can anyone ever steal from you who you fundamentally are?

There is only one who has the cunning and ability and lure to do that. He's the master con who lured the first person to sin, and the one Jesus described as "the thief [who] comes only to steal and kill and destroy" (John 10:10).

Satan, the enemy of your soul, is very focused on stealing, killing, and destroying your identity because you are made in the image of God. If he can get you to think you are no one of significance, or to believe you are no longer who you thought you were, or to make you want to be someone or something other than who you were designed to be, he can destroy you—or talk you into destroying yourself. But he is a liar. Lying accompanies stealing and killing. And he combines all three to try to make you and me forget who we are, who we ever were, and the fact that no one can ever snatch us out of our loving Father's hands.

God must have known our identities would be vulnerable to Satan's attacks and the cause of much grief to us personally if we weren't convinced of Whose we are. He certainly knew we would be very fragile at times when it came to knowing for certain who we are. Perhaps that's why there are so many descriptions in His Word reminding us, affirming us, and confirming to us who—and Whose—we really are:

- You are God's child, Jesus tells us in John 1:12.

- You are Christ's friend (John 15:15), not just an acquaintance.

- You are bought with a price (the death of God's Son) and belong to God (1 Corinthians 6:19-20).

- You are a saint (Ephesians 1:1). In Christ, you are seen as perfectly spotless, regardless of your past.

- You have been adopted as God's child (Ephesians 1:5), therefore you weren't an unplanned or unwanted child—you were *chosen*.

- You are redeemed and forgiven (seen as brand new in God's eyes, regardless of your past sins, mistakes, and failures— 2 Corinthians 5:17).

- You are complete in Christ (Colossians 2:10). That old saying, "God ain't finished with me yet" ain't true. God sees you as *already* complete, whole, and perfect because of your trust in Jesus' atonement for your sin.

- You are the light of the earth (Matthew 5:14).

- You are a branch and God is the vine (John 15:5). That's God's way of saying "You're a chip off the old block."

- You are God's temple (1 Corinthians 3:16).

- You are God's work of art (Ephesians 2:10).

- You are capable of doing all things through Christ's strength in you (Philippians 4:13).

- You are able to approach God with freedom and confidence (Ephesians 3:12).

- You are the holder of a seat with Christ in the heavenly realm (Ephesians 2:6). *You have reservations for VIP seats!*

- You are free from condemnation (Romans 8:1).

- You are established, anointed, and sealed by God (2 Corinthians 1:21-22).

- You are inseparable from God's love (Romans 8:35-39).

- You are a citizen of heaven (Philippians 3:20).

Your true identity is not based upon how you feel or what you do, or what that harsh inner critic is telling you. Your *true identity* is recorded in Scripture. God said it, nothing can change it, and no one can steal it.

Lord, help me to listen to Your voice, and not the one that tries to tell me a different narrative about who I am.

TODAY'S CHALLENGE

Choose one of the "you are" identity statements above and rephrase it using the words "I am...," and say it to at least one other person today.

PRAYING THROUGH
THE SILENCE

This is the confidence which we have before Him,
that, if we ask anything according
to His will, He hears us.
And if we know that He hears us in whatever we ask,
we know that we have the requests
which we have asked from Him.

1 JOHN 5:14-15

I'm sure you know what it's like to wait upon God for something and to wonder, at times, if He's even there.

You've prayed—over and over. But is He listening anymore?

I remember waiting upon God for a second child and wondering if He was even there during that struggle. But now I realize—nearly 30 years later and still no second child—that God knew what He was doing all along. He did hear my prayers. He did see my tears. But He had a better plan.

It's difficult to imagine how God can have a purpose or happy ending to our life's story when we're right in the middle of longing for something more or missing something we once had. But God sees our story from beginning to end and He knows exactly what He is preparing us for, even when we feel as if He isn't doing anything on our behalf.

If you're in the frustrating place of trying to get God's ear, I encourage you to hang on to three sources of hope in the midst of what might seem like unanswered prayer:

Hope in God's Word. Did you know that God cannot contradict His Word? While He has guidelines in Scripture that are not necessarily promises, there are certain passages that include promises that hold true as we obey Him. For example, 2 Corinthians 1:20 tells us, "All the promises of God in Him are Yes, and in Him Amen, to the glory of God through us" (NKJV). His Word further tells us: "This is the confidence which we have before Him, that, if we ask anything according to His will, He hears us. And if we know that He hears us in whatever we ask, we know that we have the requests which we have asked from Him." Hold God to His Word, and you have hope to hold on to as well.

Hope in God's Character. God also cannot contradict Himself. So, when He says in His Word that He causes all things to work together for good to those who love Him and are called according to His purpose (Romans 8:28), He will do just that. He will take care of what You place into His hands. The more you get to know God, the more you will trust Him. The more you trust Him, the less you will doubt, worry, fear, or give up. Psalm 62:8 further tells us: "Trust in Him at all times… Pour out your hearts before Him; God is a refuge for us." God is a refuge for our sorrows, prayers, and requests that we can't take anywhere else. And He will not tell us to pour out our hearts to Him and then not listen. He can be trusted.

Hope in God's Timing. God knows exactly when you are ready to receive the desire of your heart, and He will not act a moment too soon or a moment too late when it comes to doing what is eternally best for you.

When you are in the long haul of waiting and you aren't getting a *yes,* will you trust that what you might think is a *no* might really be God's *wait?* It's possible He has something even better for you than what you have requested. Deuteronomy 32:4 says His works are perfect and all His ways are just, and He is

> The more you get to know God, the more you will trust Him. The more you trust Him, the less you will doubt, worry, fear, or give up.

"a faithful God who does no wrong" (NLT). He knows best. Therefore, His timing is always perfect.

Keep hoping in Him, my friend. Hope in His Word, His character, and His timing. He hears your prayers, He sees your tears, and He can be trusted with your heart.

Maker of my heart, nothing goes unnoticed before You. Even when I think there is only silence, You are still there, You still hear, and You are still working on my behalf. Thank You for Your great love for me. May I please Your heart by trusting in You and the unseen work of Your hands. In the precious name of Jesus, I pray this. Amen.

TODAY'S CHALLENGE

Focus on Who God is and not what you want from Him. In the space below (or in a journal), write out everything you can praise and thank Him for, even if it appears He is not answering that one request on your heart.

LISTENING TO THE RIGHT VOICE

*My sheep listen to My voice,
and I know them, and they follow Me.*

John 10:27

*A*re you listening to the gentle voice of your Loving Shepherd, who knows how to guide, nourish, and protect His sheep? Or is that harsh inner critic talking a little too loudly for you to hear the truth about who you really are and Who loves you?

We all hear that critical voice now and then telling us what we've done wrong, what we can't seem to get right, what we might as well not try because we'll just mess it up. That voice taunts us, shames us, belittles us. But we don't have to listen to those thoughts. Many times, they aren't even our own.

The psalmist experienced this inner critic when he penned Psalm 42: "Why am I discouraged? Why is my heart so sad?" he asked himself in verse 5 (NLT). He couldn't seem to get out of his despondency. Then he did what we all need to do. He straightened out his derailed mindset by immediately telling himself what to do and how to think: "Put your hope in God, for I will yet praise him, my Savior and my God" (verse 5 NIV).

Is your inner critic telling you that you are not measuring up to the standard at work? Is it convincing you that you are failing at home? Is it taunting you about not living up to your personal potential or fulfilling your purpose? Maybe it's persuading you that you pale in comparison to all those women on Instagram or that those you love the most are deeply disappointed in you.

Perhaps your critic is accusing you of having no friends and of being a failure socially.

Oh, the lies we tell ourselves. And the ways we shame ourselves. When we do, we allow the enemy of our soul to gain traction in our thoughts, rather than letting God whisper His affirmations into our ear and soothe our perceived inadequacies with His words of comfort and assurance.

Considering all that is written about who God says we are in Him, why do we still tend to believe the negative words that run through our minds?

But that's who you used to be, not who you are now.

But that was before you messed up.

It's different now—you're not the beloved child of God that you used to be.

Oh, my friend, as real and convincing as those thoughts may sound at times, you were not the exception when the psalmist wrote: "As far as the east is from the west, so far has He removed our wrongdoings from us" (Psalm 103:12).

You were not left out when Jesus affirmed to His followers, "I have called you friends" (John 15:15).

You were not excluded when Jesus, who proclaimed He was *the Light* of the world (John 8:12) gave you one of the greatest compliments there is by saying you, too, are the light of the world (Matthew 5:14). (You and

I are *flashlights* of the world compared to Him, the Spotlight. He was saying you are a representative, an ambassador, His mini-me, reflecting His pure light and truth.)

Can you believe the solid truth of the words of God today, instead of listening to the random thoughts that enter your mind or the predictable, age-old voice that always gets it wrong?

If you have bouts of feeling unworthy, my friend, you *are*. So am I. That's why Jesus came. He knew all of us were stained by a sin nature, incapable of pleasing God and living up to His standard. But He dealt with our unworthiness once and for all on the cross and now commands us to live in our *new* nature, the one He gifted to us with His precious blood. You and I can get over the fact that we're unworthy by embracing it and letting it propel us to deeper praise. Because of the worthiness of Jesus' accomplishment on the cross, we are worthy to be called children of God: "Behold what manner of love the Father has bestowed on us, that we should be called children of God!" (1 John 3:1 NKJV).

The realization of our worthiness in Him should cause you and me to hear a different voice each day…the voice of the One who calls us His own.

What do you need to tell your inner critic today? What do you need to say aloud to yourself or to the enemy of your soul, who is trying to gain some headway in your thinking? Try some of these proclamations, all of which are personalized paraphrases of Scripture:

"I am loved with an everlasting love!" (see Jeremiah 31:3).

"I am forgiven by God's rich grace that He lavished on me!" (see Ephesians 1:7-8).

"I am chosen in Him!" (see Ephesians 1:11).

As you recite God's descriptions of you, you will be tuning your ears to the frequency of *His* voice, and you will know in an instant which voices stem from His love and truth, and which ones are not worth listening to.

> *Lord Jesus, may Your sweet words and Your gentle voice drown out the destructive thoughts and critical voices in my mind.*

TODAY'S CHALLENGE

Every hour on the hour, write down—or say aloud—one loving truth about how God feels toward you.

HIS INCREDIBLE RESCUES

My mouth will tell of your righteous deeds,
of your saving acts all day long—
though I know not how to relate them all.

PSALM 71:15 NIV

How often I'm in need of a rescue—physically, as well as behaviorally, emotionally, and relationally.

- I start to change lanes on the freeway by checking my rear-view mirror only (instead of looking over my shoulder), and then I see the truck barreling closer in my blind spot that would've tossed me across the lanes like a matchbox car.

- I begin to blurt out something I'll later regret, and then God's Spirit hushes me like a divine hand over my mouth so I will think before I speak.

- I start to feel sorry for myself, and then the Lord brings to my mind unfathomable blessings that I have so easily taken for granted, which keeps me from nurturing a victim mindset.

Oh, the rescues I need—and the ones God has already performed that I might not have even noticed.

Can you relate?

King David, a man who needed—and was familiar with—many rescues, says this of the God who always had his back: "All day long I will tell the wonderful things you do to save your people. But you have done much more than I could possibly know" (Psalm 71:15 CEV).

How much more has He done than you and I could possibly know?

Was He the One who caused that strikingly handsome yet unbelieving man who wanted to date you to suddenly move out of state with no way for you to reach him?

Was He the One who allowed you to miss that exit—and then meander through a frustrating ten-minute detour—so you wouldn't be on the road at the precise time of that three-car pileup?

Was He the One who delayed your plane—or cancelled your flight—so you wouldn't be in the air during those dangerous weather conditions or that mechanical failure?

Was He the One who told that man to stop you as you drove out of the car wash because your wallet was on the ground and you needed your ID to board a plane early the next morning?

Those rescues have all happened to me, leaving me speechless at the way God intervened to avert what would have been sure disaster.

Then there are the times God saves us, and we attribute it to something or someone else:

- "Good thing my smoke alarm went off, or I wouldn't have known about the oven fire downstairs."

- "Thank goodness we installed those new locks on our doors, or we might have been burglarized as several of our neighbors were."

- "I guess I'll never know what could've happened in that relationship because I never got a chance to explore it."

Yet in Psalm 4:8, David tells us who ultimately is handling our safety detail: "for you alone, O Lord, make me dwell in safety" (ESV).

God saves our souls once for all eternity. But He continues to save us "all day long" in our circumstances, our choices, and our attitudes.

In the margin of my Bible next to Psalm 71:15, I listed what I need to be saved from all day long:

- my anxious thoughts

- motives that don't glorify God

- fear of what I can't control

- resentments that start to take root in my heart

- pride in my accomplishments, as if they were "mine"

- a preoccupation with self

- careless decisions made without prayer

- a critical mindset

- too many words flowing out of me (*O Lord, put a filter on my mouth!*)

- a love for this world that competes with love for my Lord

What do you need to be saved from all day long? A sharp tongue? An impatient spirit? A lack of attention to those who need you most? A complacency toward the One who loves you more than you can fathom?

Pay attention to what is happening around you and start recording your "salvation all day long" as a result of God's watchful eye on you.

Perhaps your gift back to Him for His rescues is that you *can* recount them all, even ones you would have ordinarily missed.

Lord, thank You for continually saving me all day long—from my circumstances, from my carelessness, and from myself. For You alone, O Lord, make me dwell in safety. May the desire of my heart be to continually recount to others all that You have done for me and those I love.

TODAY'S CHALLENGE

Ask God to open your eyes to His rescues all day long. Then start a running list of them—in the space below, in a journal, in your Bible next to Psalm 71:15, or on one of your devices.

Lord, thank You for rescuing me from these situations:

DISSOLVING FEAR AND WORRY

*All my days were written in Your book and
planned before a single one of them began.*

Psalm 139:16 hcsb

I sat on my back patio thinking about something I've dreaded
for a while.

*God, please don't take Dad anytime soon. I can't imagine
life on Earth without him.*

My father, now 87 years old, had always been in great health. His
parents lived into their 90s. A first-generation full-blooded Swede born
in America, he and his family worked the land as organic farmers and
lived on whole foods practically their entire lives. Yet cancer is no discriminator of persons. And prostate cancer is no discriminator when it
comes to men. Five years after radiation treatments that barely slowed
him down, but greatly slowed down the cancer, Dad is now experiencing rising numbers and a recurrence of the prostate cancer threat. And
now, he is too old to qualify for the next stage of treatment.

I used to be afraid my dad would die with unresolved issues between the two of us. But through the years, I have seen God transform my father from the inside out, and he has become my loving dad, mentor, and friend. Although we live 300 miles apart, I visit a few times a year, and he and I now talk on the phone weekly. I love hearing his stories of people in town he is ministering to, of the prayer groups and Bible studies he is still attending, of the divine appointments he would have driving people here and there as the "unofficial Uber driver" in the small town where he raised me.

> Nothing touches you—or those you love—that hasn't first passed through His loving hands.

He is no longer driving now. He walks slower and is much more tired. Age is catching up to him quickly. And sometimes that makes me fearful.

"God, don't let Dad go yet," I found myself praying again this morning. "Please let him live at least as long as his parents did."

And then the gentle voice I've come to discern as my Heavenly Father's spoke to my heart.

I appointed his days before any of them came to be.

My Father in heaven appointed the day my father on Earth would be born, and my God knows the exact day my dad will pass from Earth as well. God doesn't just know. He *appointed* it. Before Dad was born. God knows exactly what He's doing in each of our lives, and He will orchestrate the transition of you and me and our loved ones into the next life. Psalm 116:15 assures me, "Precious in the sight of the LORD is the death of His godly ones."

Still, I can't imagine life one day without Dad. Without him being a phone call away. Without visiting him when I return to my hometown. Without hearing him call me "Ceenee" or asking me, teasingly, to still be his daughter for "two more days."

As I laid before God my fear of losing Dad, my understanding solidified that death in this life is inevitable, but it is also the sweet transition into the physical arms of our Savior.

In my thinking, Dad must hang on longer because I'm not ready to say goodbye. In God's goodness, perhaps He will take Dad home sooner because He knows best.

Trust Me with the beginnings and the ends, and everything in between, my Lord spoke to my heart.

Today, the fear of losing my dad dissolved into a deeper trust of my Heavenly Father. God is so wise. He is so good. He is so loving. And according to Psalm 18:30, all His ways are perfect, and that includes His timing and the method by which He chooses to take every one of us home. Because the death of His loved ones is "precious" in His sight, it is no small matter to Him how and when He takes those He loves, and how long they live on this earth to love us.

Instead of worrying or fearing about the timing of a loss or how it might occur, I fall into Jesus' arms and trust Him more. And I receive His unexplainable peace.

Who—or what—are you afraid of losing today? Can you trust your concern is in the tender hands of your Savior, whose timing and ways are perfect? Nothing touches you—or those you love—that hasn't first passed through His loving hands. Trust His goodness, His wisdom, and His love. He will be there to comfort you when the time comes.

Thank You, Heavenly Father, for knowing what's best for me, as well as for those I love. Calm my heart with the knowledge that You make no mistakes, and that, in Your eyes, nothing is an accident. I trust Your goodness, wisdom, and love.

TODAY'S CHALLENGE

Give to God whatever concerns you today. He already knows about it, but He wants you to come to Him like a daughter seeking the comfort and advice of a loving father.

WHEN LOVE SPEAKS LOUDER THAN FEAR

You will keep in perfect peace all who trust in you, all whose thoughts are fixed on you!

Isaiah 26:3 nlt

I remember the day I first realized that my concern for my dad had turned to fear.

Why am I consumed with fear if my trust is in You, O Lord?

Forty years earlier, I feared losing him because there were unresolved issues in our relationship. My fear was more that he would take his life because he was at a very low point, and I would live with regrets that he and I hadn't worked things out, or that I never had the father I needed. I feared I would experience what many women go through in an estranged or hurtful relationship (or no relationship) with their father. At that time, part of my fear of losing Dad was that I also believed he would never change. At one point, I found myself arrogantly and foolishly thinking, *Not even God can change him.*

But God transformed my father from the inside out. On his

thirty-ninth sobriety birthday, I called him on the phone and told him I used to fear that he would die with unresolved issues still between us, but today I fear losing him because I don't want to be without my loving daddy. I told him how thankful I was to God for the many ways in which he has changed and become more like Jesus through the years. I told him I was proud of him for completely surrendering his life to the Lord and faithfully following the steps in his recovery program and, as a result, becoming an inspiration and encouragement to so many in his church and community. I sensed healing in that conversation, for both of us. Dad was touched by my words. But still, the fear remained that I would lose him one day, and the pain would be unbearable.

> He is more than capable of guiding us through what we think we won't be able to handle.

The morning after I saw the ultrasound image of a tumor on my thyroid, I called Dad, feeling a bit fearful for *my* life this time. Dad was at one of his prayer groups when he answered the phone and told me I called at the perfect time. He and some men were about to spend time in prayer, and he said he would lift me up to God that morning. When I got off the phone, I said aloud, "Thank You, God, that I have a dad who is still alive who loves and cares so much about me." As soon as I spoke those words, the tears began to fall. And I felt God impress upon my heart the message, *I'm your Dad who loves and cares about you even more, and you'll never, ever lose Me.*

In that moment, I realized that if God can comfort me as I thank Him that my earthly father is still alive, He can surely comfort me when the day comes that my earthly father goes to meet Him—because I have a faithful Daddy God who will never, ever leave. He can comfort you during such times too.

A year later, when I was no longer tormented by the thought of losing my dad, I rather unexpectedly lost my mom. I flew across the country to visit and care for her for two weeks, but she passed only a week after I arrived. Yet God had prepared me for that week in ways I hadn't anticipated. He had orchestrated the timing of her passing so I would be there to hold her hand, and He graciously met me at each step I thought I couldn't take. He covered every detail of her dying moments, giving her the pain-free death surrounded by her children that she had prayed for, while giving to my siblings and me what we each needed emotionally during those last few days of her life.

Today I don't fear my dad's death because of how God showed Himself strong in every detail of my mom's. Though my parents, divorced for years, lived on different sides of the country, God brought all things together in His will and His way, and soothed the hurt in my heart that could've been so prevalent.

God is intimately aware of our greatest fears and our deepest feelings of loss. And He is more than capable of guiding us through what we think we won't be able to handle. Will you let Him into those fears and trust that He can provide for you in whatever you don't believe you can live through? I believe the breaks in our hearts from loss or anxious thoughts produce the cracks through which His love seeps in, soothes, and heals.

Lord, Your love is so much greater than any fear or loss that threatens to topple me. And You cradle in Your loving hands what is most important to me. Thank You that You are capable of carrying me through.

TODAY'S CHALLENGE

Release your fears and anxious thoughts at the moment they start to bombard you by whispering these words aloud: "Jesus, take this fear—and pain—and replace it with Your peace."

WHATEVER YOU WISH

*Whatever you ask in My name, this I will do, so
that the Father may be glorified in the Son. If you
ask Me anything in My name, I will do it.*

John 14:13-14

esus gave us an extraordinary promise in John 14:13-14 that
takes the work and duty out of prayer and makes it an intimate component of our relationship with the Lover of our
soul: "If you ask Me anything in My name, I will do it."

Anything?

That's a pretty bold promise from Jesus. If one of His children asks
anything in His name, He will do it.

I can ask that I win the contest?

I can ask that He give me a husband?

I can ask that He help me get pregnant, or get this job, or qualify
for that house?

Psalm 37:4 is a treasured verse that I believe holds the secret to seeing God answer our every request: "Delight yourself in the Lord; and

He will give you the desires of your heart." Some Bible versions simplify that verse to read: "Do what the Lord wants, and he will give you your heart's desire" (cev) and "Enjoy serving the Lord, and he will give you what you want" (ncv). But those renderings make it sound like it's up to us and what we *do* in order to get what we want from God. Because the majority of Bible versions translate the verse in some variation of "Take delight in the Lord," we can see it's more about our hearts and who comes first.

Psalm 37:4 isn't saying to ask whatever you want, and God will give it to you. Our all-knowing Heavenly Father wisely knows we need boundaries around what our hearts seek after. And much of what we request, unbeknownst to us, may not be for our eternal good, or our earthly best. James 4:3 says, "You ask and do not receive, because you ask with the wrong motives, so that you may spend what you request on your pleasures."

There is a beautiful clarification in Psalm 37:4, and in all of Jesus' instructions on prayer, that we can easily miss. And it's all about our motives.

When David encouraged us to "delight" ourselves in the Lord and He will give us the desires of our hearts, the emphasis is on the first part of the verse (how we pray) and how it impacts the second part of it (how He responds). As we *delight* in Him, as we make Him our primary desire, He places *His* desires in our hearts, which He will delight in granting.

What a good, good Father He is to prime His children for what to ask, because He already has it stored up for us.

Dr. Lloyd John Ogilvie wrote, "Long before we thought of praying, the God to whom we pray was preparing us to pray. Our prayer is response. When a need comes to our mind and we pray, it is because God [already] has an answer to give us for that concern."[4]

Prayer is an important part of our relationship with God. He realizes that as we ask and He answers, our trust for Him deepens. But He wants us to know *what* to ask for, and that comes through intimately abiding with Him—taking the time to hear His voice, to develop a stronger love for Him, to share His desires.

In John 15:7, Jesus further said, "If you remain in Me, and My words remain in you, ask whatever you wish, and it will be done for you." There it is again. *Whatever you wish*. But that promise of *whatever* is dependent upon our remaining in Him and His words remaining in us. As we draw closer to the Lover of our soul, His desires become our desires, and eventually, our desires (and what we ask for in prayer) become His delight.

The promise, if we were to break it down into a few practical steps, looks like this:

1. Remain in Jesus.

2. Keep His words in you.

3. Ask whatever you wish.

4. Whatever you ask will be done.

Ogilvie said Jesus gives us two big "ifs" for dynamic praying. *If* we abide—that's the essence of prayer and knowing what to ask for. And *if* we ask in His name—that's the element of effectiveness in our prayer.[5]

To ask for something *in Jesus' name* does not mean to merely add that phrase to the end of your request. It means to ask God the Father for something that Jesus Himself would ask for. It is to ask on behalf of the Savior—God's beloved Son—just as Jesus prayed while on this earth for all He needed on behalf of His Father, and the work His Father wanted Him to accomplish.

Precious Heavenly Father, lay on my heart what You want me to ask for, and then give me the power to ask boldly. May my prayers be a delight for You to answer.

TODAY'S CHALLENGE

Ask God, throughout this day, to put His desires for your life and the lives of others on your heart, and to remind you to pray for them.

NO CONDEMNATION, ONLY GRACE

How far has the LORD taken our sins from us?
Farther than the distance from east to west!

PSALM 103:12 CEV

*O*n those days when the enemy of your soul, or your own destructive thoughts, bring back to your mind the sins of your past, remember: God has removed your sins from as far as the east is from the west.

During times when you feel you can't approach God because you are still struggling with an addiction or a habitual sin, remember: "There is no condemnation for those who belong to Christ Jesus" (Romans 8:1 NLT). He is the One who sent His Spirit to indwell you and help you through those struggles. He will not sit back and judge you for them.

When you start to feel unworthy to come before God's presence, or even whisper a prayer, remember, you are *not* worthy. You never *will* be. *None* of us are. That is why Jesus had to come. Our worth and righteousness is found in Him once we receive Him as the Savior of our sin who takes care of all our unworthiness, diseases of self, dysfunctions, addictions, and anything else that would keep us from God. And if you know Him and have His Spirit in you (which happened at the moment of your salvation), nothing can keep you from God. Not your memories of where you came from, not your shameful thoughts, not your actions last night, not your guilt. Nothing.

Romans 8, which starts out telling us there is no condemnation for those who belong to Christ, ends by saying, "Neither death, nor life, nor angels, nor principalities, nor things present, nor things to come, nor powers, nor height, nor depth, nor any other created thing will be able to separate us from the love of God that is in Christ Jesus our Lord" (verses 38-39). So, there's no reason to sink in shame or grovel in guilt.

On the day you feel too ashamed to once again call upon the name of the Lord, remember that you are *already* healed and made whole in Him.

Reflect on Scripture's prescription for your brokenness and every failure you will ever make:

> It was our sicknesses that He Himself bore,
> and our pains that He carried…
> He was pierced for our offenses,
> He was crushed for our wrongdoings;
> the punishment for our well-being was laid upon
> Him,
> and by His wounds we are healed" (Isaiah 53:4-5).

Did you notice that every verb in those verses is *past tense* except for in the last sentence, which says we *are* healed? That means back when the prophet Isaiah foretold what Jesus would do centuries later to heal and redeem us, God saw our healing as *already* done, even though Jesus hadn't yet been born. This also means that way back before we were born, God saw us as *already* healed even before we had ever sinned. God saw Jesus' work already completed for an eternity to those He chose to follow Him. Think about that. You are *already* healed spiritually in Christ Jesus, and your Father in heaven sees you as completely whole, not a complete mess.

With that credit on your account, that favor in your court, that redemption story as the theme of your life, how can you keep lowering your head in shame and not lift it toward heaven in praise for the unconditional love and irreversible grace He has shown you?

This God, who knows and remembers everything, specifically tells us in His Word there is *one* thing He does not remember or keep record of: our sin. God has no weakness or disability, yet has *chosen* to do something that we, as humans, see as a weakness: forget. He *chooses* to forget our sin. We see forgetfulness as a weakness and failing, but God's ability to forget our sin is one of His mightiest strengths and proofs of His love. He forgives and forgets when it comes to our sin. Oh, that we could do the same.

Each time you remember a sin, give it to God again. He'll respond, *What is this you keep bringing back to Me? I forgot what this was. Certainly, I've already dealt with this. Let's talk about what's ahead for you in this new life I've given you, not what is irrelevant and behind you.* And He will then fill you with His peace that always follows prayer.

Give it all to Him. Then move on. He already has—into what you will do next with His strength. Give Jesus credit for what He accomplished on the cross and enter new territory—what you are determined to forget, and leave behind, so you can become more like Him.

Thank You, precious Jesus, that I am already healed and whole in Your sight. Help me to live out my new identity—one who is complete in Christ Jesus. And don't ever let me shrink back from bringing my heart to You.

TODAY'S CHALLENGE

Focus on remembering God's forgiveness and forgetting your sin. He is looking ahead to your glorious future of becoming more like Him. It's time you do that too.

PART II

CONNECTING WITH ONE ANOTHER

LOSING THE GUILT

*There is no condemnation for those
who belong to Christ.*

ROMANS 8:1 NLT

*A*re you sinking under a to-do list that grows longer every night—ever aware of what you need to be doing, but finding little time to do it?

In talking with numerous women in their late 20s and early 30s, I was saddened at how pressured they felt, in addition to everything else on their plates, to "do the right things" to live the Christian life they felt God and others expected.

"I need to develop deep friendships with other women I can be open and honest with, but how do I do that?" one young woman in her late 20s asked me recently.

"I know I need to have a Christian community, a place where I can share my struggles and grow alongside others, but where do I find that, and where do I get the time?" another expressed.

"I need to spend more time in the Bible and in prayer, and I feel so guilty every time I don't," said a full-time working mom who has a toddler.

We not only long to be known and to live in close connection with others, but we feel mounting guilt over not spending enough time with God, not being in His Word long enough, not cultivating a relationship with Him first and then with others. The need for authenticity and a sense of genuine community with one another is apparently one of the most compelling needs of believers today.

Jesus understands. He's seen it all before. He sees it now. And the words He spoke centuries ago to those who were struggling under the heavy demands of the religious system still resonate with our busy, overwhelmed lives today, and our hearts that are hungry for more:

> Come to me, all of you who are weary and carry heavy burdens, and I will give you rest. Take my yoke upon you. Let me teach you, because I am humble and gentle at heart, and you will find rest for your souls. For my yoke is easy to bear, and the burden I give you is light (Matthew 11:28-30 NLT).

The people of Jesus' day were trying to follow every rule, be good enough for God, not sink under the weight of numerous expectations of the law and cultural legalism. Jesus' words, like a salve to their overburdened souls, can bring healing to you, too, right where you are.

Jesus came to give us a life of more abundance, not a life of more guilt. Could it be that what you perceive as guilt is actually the gentle nudging by your Savior to spend some quiet reflective time with Him? Could your feelings of guilt (from not attending a church, perhaps?) be His pull for you to connect with other believers so you can grow spiritually? He wants you to flourish as a believer, not feel like a failure. He wants to help you get to where He designed you to be in your personal and spiritual life, and He wants you to not feel overburdened by all you believe you must *do*. It's not so much about getting it right as it is about not being overburdened.

Lay your feelings of inadequacy before Him. He knows your heart, your schedule, and your needs. He also knows your weaknesses and failures, which can be open doors to a more intimate relationship with Him. No one wants a friend to visit out of obligation. Neither does God want you coming to Him solely out of duty. Come because He is your soul's wellspring of water. Come because, in His presence, there is fullness of joy and at His right hand there are pleasures forever (Psalm 16:11).

Be willing to simply take the time to sit with Him and open your heart, and see what He opens to you in return. It may start with a Jesus-following friend who enters your life, or a call from a family member or loved one inviting you to church or to an event. It may be one passage of Scripture that pours soothing oil on your soul. Or it may be a few moments in which you remember He loves you and will equip you with all you need to get through your day.

While statistics show that most people today between the ages of 25 to 35 no longer see the local church as relevant, Jesus said your participation in it is essential to living an obedient and flourishing life in Him. If God hasn't done so already, pray that He will lead you to a body of believers, and then be willing to follow His lead and commit. The church is, by definition, the "body" (human manifestation) of Christ—individuals saved by His grace who gather to celebrate who He is and the eternal hope and life He's given them. Find a way to be a part of that celebration so you, too, can grow and develop into the woman He designed you to be.

Lord, draw me closer to You. Bring people into my life who can help fine-tune my heart and encourage me to grow. Show me where my spiritual community is and grow me into Your plan and purpose for my life. Thank You for Your unconditional love for me.

TODAY'S CHALLENGE

Throughout the day, ask God to help you prioritize what matters most and to let the rest go, without guilt.

THE DANGER OF ISOLATION

Whoever isolates himself seeks his own desire;
he breaks out against all sound judgment.

Proverbs 18:1 esv

Life can get busy, and we can easily find ourselves isolating from one another. We may not intend to isolate, but when our to-do list screams at us to be more productive, the needs from our family become too insistent, and our internal cry is to get away from everyone, the natural reaction can sometimes be to shut others out.

We can also shut others out as a way of protecting ourselves from possibly being hurt. But have you considered that detaching yourself from other believers might actually *increase* your chances of harm?

Setting aside time for solitude, to be alone with God and your thoughts, is healthy. But isolation—walling yourself off from others, or simply thinking you are fine on your own—is dangerous.

While I was visiting my brother, Dan, in North Africa, we were walking through a park when he called my attention to something I had never seen in the States. He pointed to small caterpillars—dark grey and black in color—traveling single file, one after another, linked so closely that they looked like one long snake to any predator lurking above them.

"When they link up with one another, they appear bigger and more powerful than they are, and they are protected from birds or other animals who would otherwise eat them," Dan said. "They stick close to each other as their defense." I watched the creatures closely. They weren't crawling about independently, doing their own thing and coming together only when they needed something to do or eat. Unification was their mode of operation. They stuck together for their survival.

In Proverbs 6:6-8, Solomon instructs us to look at the ant and gain wisdom from her work ethic. We ought to look also to the caterpillars in North Africa to gain wisdom from their survival skills. When we link up with other believers, we're less of a target to our enemy. We are protected as we are among each other and cooperating. We are not to be renegade, off by ourselves, doing what is right in our own eyes. Once we separate and go our own way, we become fodder for the enemy.

In Scripture, we are given more than 30 "one-another" commands, instructing us how to live with and relate to other believers as we link up with them. We are not to link up only when it's time for a potluck or a church-related event. We are to *live* linked, unified, as a mode of operation. It's our defense. But like the caterpillars, when you and I are alone, we are prey to the enemy.

Satan, the enemy of your soul, knows the potential of a like-minded believer to strengthen your faith. Therefore, he wants you to believe you're fine on your own, you're strong independently, and that no one really has time to hear of your struggles anyway. If he can get you alone in your thoughts, he can bring in shame about your past, doubt about your present, and fear about your future. He will also try to lure you toward destructive thoughts about yourself and others.

Think about it. When people are alone, they get depressed. When people are alone, they damage their bodies. When people are alone, they contemplate taking their lives. Satan strikes the believer when she is alone. Therefore, he wants nothing more than for you to detach from the train of believers and move increasingly further from the body of Christ, and to believe God's church is no longer relevant to you today. But God created us to be dependent on Him and *inter*dependent on one another so we can live in community with one another and He can be glorified in our celebrations as well as our sufferings.

King Solomon, who was known as the wisest man who ever lived, started Proverbs 18 telling us that when we isolate ourselves we are seeking our own desire, not considering the wisdom of others.

In another translation, that verse reads: "Whoever pulls away from others to focus solely on his own desires disregards any sense of sound judgment" (The Voice).

Solomon also gave us this wisdom in Ecclesiastes 4:9-12:

> Two are better than one because they have a good return for their labor; for if either of them falls, the one will lift up his companion. But woe to the one who falls when there is not another to lift him up! Furthermore, if two lie down together they keep warm, but how can one be warm alone? And if one can overpower him who is alone, two can resist him. A cord of three strands is not quickly torn apart.

Solomon was saying there is strength in numbers—when we surround ourselves with believers.

God designed us to live in community. Don't try to go it alone, my friend. Link up with others who are on this journey with you. You need them for your spiritual survival as much as they need you.

Lord, thank You for the lessons that exist in nature. Help me to be wise and to link up with other believers so I will stay strong in You and never try to walk alone.

TODAY'S CHALLENGE

Who can you spend time with this week as a step toward linking up with another believer?

GETTING REAL

You have looked deep into my heart, LORD,
and you know all about me.

PSALM 139:1 CEV

ur cry is for authenticity. Oh, to be our genuine selves and know others as they truly are, not as they appear to be on their social media pages, online dating profiles, or behind a screen. In a day of artificial intelligence and online "relationships," how do we know someone is who they say they are? How can we trust the people we meet online or the "friend" who messages us from what could be a hacked social media account?

And how do we know who to trust with *our* authentic selves? What if we let our guard down and we end up being sorry we did? Is God the only one who really is who His Word says He is?

God lovingly makes Himself known to us through His Word, through His comforting and enabling presence, and through His love expressed to us by other believers. And He longs for us to be authentic with Him and others in the body of Christ.

Yet He understands our fears. He knows the inner workings of our hearts and is the only one who knows us far better than we know ourselves. We tend to see ourselves through the lenses of what we'd prefer to see, or of how others have seen us. We often define ourselves by the labels we've been given, or with medical or psychological terms that describe our disabilities, weaknesses, phobias, and mental and emotional frailties. Yet as we trust in Jesus, God's love covers our inadequacies and He sees us as perfect, like His sinless Son.

At the end of Psalm 139, after singing of all God knows about him, David then invited God to look further: "Look deep into my heart, God, and find out everything I am thinking" (verse 23 cev). David wasn't holding anything back. "And see if there is any hurtful [or idolatrous]* way in me, and lead me in the everlasting way" (verse 24). David wanted his Creator to examine everything that lurked within him and to clear out what needed to go so he could be all that God desired.

Does anyone else besides God truly know you? If so, you are blessed. I remember, during a lonely season of my life, believing there was *no one* who really knew me. And if they did, they certainly wouldn't love me. Therefore, I believed I must still pretend to be who I never was. The thought that no one would ever truly know me was devastating. But it was also a lie from the pit of hell. A lie that Satan, the enemy of my soul—and yours—wants us to believe so we will feel rejected, defeated, and without hope. He wants to belittle us so much that we refuse to believe our loving Creator knew exactly what we'd be like and still He created us, saved us, and continues to love us.

"Where can I go from your Spirit? Where can I flee from your

---

* Both the New English Translation and the Contemporary English Bible translate the Hebrew word for *hurtful*, *evil*, or *wicked* to our English word *idolatrous*.

presence?" the psalmist asked in verse 7. And then in verses 8-10, he answered with God-breathed words:

> If I go up to *the heavens*, you are there;
> if I make my bed *in the depths*, you are there.
>
> If I rise on the wings of the dawn,
> if I settle *on the far side of the sea,*
>
> even there your hand will guide me,
> your right hand will hold me fast (verses 8-10 NIV).

Are you in *the heavens* (or on top of the world) right now, trying to keep it all together so you can maintain your relationships with those whom you believe love you for how successful you are?

Have you sunk to *the depths* of despair, where you believe no one wants to be around you anymore?

Have you settled *on the far side of the sea* by going into your cave and walling yourself off so no one can get in and hurt you again?

Even there, Scripture says, you are not hidden from the God who loves you and will continue to guide you and hold you with His right hand.

Don't let go of God's right hand. He is your lifeline. And He can bring to your mind—and to your door—the people who love you for who you really are.

Thank You, Lord Jesus, that "all my ways are known to you" (Psalm 119:168 NIV) and yet You love me still. Help me to feel safe being real with You and to take the risk of being real with others, knowing You have my back and my name.

TODAY'S CHALLENGE

If you have a friend who truly knows you, thank God for that friend and send her a message letting her know how much you appreciate her. If you don't yet feel you have a friend who truly knows you, ask God to bring her into your life or reveal to you who that person is who is *already* in your life.

WHEN YOU'VE DISAPPOINTED SOMEONE

You know when I sit down and when I get up;
You understand my thought from far away…
and are acquainted with all my ways.

PSALM 139:2-3

I t's one thing to be disappointed in someone. It's entirely another thing when someone is disappointed in you. And yet, it's par for the course in a world of misunderstandings, accusations, and mistakes on our part and the part of others. Sometimes you disappoint someone simply because you can't possibly please everyone.

It helps when we understand we will never be able to please *all* the people *all* the time. Most of us disappoint others as often as someone else disappoints us.

I remember sitting across the table from a friend and hearing her tearful account of the many ways I had let her down. I hadn't called her in quite a while, I had failed to extend toward her in the way she had hoped when she was going through a difficult time, and we hadn't gotten together as often as we used to.

I had hurt her. And in hearing about it, I was hurt.

Although I hate disappointing people, it seems to happen more and more as my responsibilities in ministry increase and my opportunities for social time diminish. Perhaps you can relate.

For me, there is nothing more frustrating than to realize if I had to do it over again, I wouldn't have known what to do differently to *not* hurt certain people. After I met with that friend, I ended up crying out to God, "I give up! I don't want one more conversation with a friend who is going to tell me how I've disappointed her. I don't know what to do anymore to keep people happy."

It was one of those days when one complaint felt like a million—when one person's unhappiness with me represented the whole world's disappointment with me. Again, have you been there?

As I cried out to God, I found comfort in the fact that He knows me inside and out, motives included, and ultimately, He is the One who pleads my case. Through the years, I've learned that it helps to keep these four points in mind when you've clearly disappointed someone.

1. ***Realize that misunderstandings happen.*** We all hear, funnel, and filter things differently, and that can lead to a myriad of misunderstandings between friends.

2. ***Thank Jesus that He can see your heart.*** It is comforting to know that God is familiar with all our ways and knows what we're going to say before we say it (Psalm 139:1-4). He sees our hearts, knows our intentions, and knows every time we mean well but don't express it, every time we mess

up but didn't intend to, every time we're misunderstood and miserable. He knows. And He extends grace anyway.

3. ***See it as a chance to grow.*** In addition to knowing your heart, God is also able to show you, through your situation, how you can be more loving and sensitive to the needs of others, and at the same time, not be someone who weighs down others with a list of unmet expectations.

4. ***Do what you can, and then let it go***. Sometimes there's only so much we can do. Do it. And then let it go. In my case, I wrote a card to my hurting friend and mailed it that day. I reiterated the hurt in my heart that I had caused her pain. I reminded her that I truly loved her. And then I left the matter in the Lord's hands as I prayed for her heart to receive the card well. He gave me the strength to move forward and not become bitter at her response or too timid to reach out to another person.

Whenever something hurts (like a comment, or an insult, or an unintentional offense on your part), I ask God to show me through it how I can be more sensitive next time, how I can avoid repeating the situation, or how I can become more like Christ through it. He honors our prayers when we seek to know Him better through our circumstances.

In my case, I prayed for a heart that would be more concerned with others and what they're going through than my own to-do list. And I made a conscious decision that day to extend a bit further and call more frequently when it came to that friend.

Do you sometimes feel ready to quit because you can't seem to get it right when it comes to relationships? Take heart, my friend. There is

One who knows your heart and your hurts, and your intentions and oversights. And with all He knows, He continues to give you another chance, mold you into the person He wants you to be, and show you how to imitate His love, whether it is well received or not.

Lord, I feel alone when I'm misunderstood or when I haven't been the best friend I could be. Comfort me with the knowledge that You know me, inside and out, and love me just the same.

TODAY'S CHALLENGE

If a misunderstanding exists between you and another person, pour your heart out to God about it. Ask for God's wisdom concerning what you can do to mend that situation with your friend, and let God be the One to clear your name.

HELPING THEM GET HOME

*Two are better than one because they have a
good return for their labor; for if either of them
falls, the one will lift up his companion.*

Ecclesiastes 4:9-10 nasb

riendships can be challenging. Personality differences, wounds from our past that trigger hurtful responses, and whether or not we are surrendered to the Holy Spirit's control on any given day can all contribute to relationship struggles, offenses that sting, and hurtful situations that lead us into a season of loneliness.

Yet when we find a Jesus-following friend we "mesh" with, one with whom we share common ground and can talk for hours and still look forward to the next get-together, that is truly a gift from God. I believe God orchestrates those divine appointments that develop into deep friendships. My friends who have an unwavering passion for Jesus are the ones I've been able to keep the strongest bonds with through the years. Perhaps because the bonds in Christ are the ones that last. They can be tested and tried, but they are not easily broken (Ecclesiastes 4:12).

Although Pam and I grew up in the same town, we didn't meet until we were adults. Today she is one of my sisters in Christ whom I can go years without seeing and then pick up with immediately again. What drew us together? Our common love for the Lord, His Word, and growing spiritually. These traits in common overshadowed our differences in age and background. Shortly after we met, Pam told me, "I long to sit at your feet and learn from you." Today, I say that to her. She started out thinking of me, five years younger than her, as a spiritual mentor in her life. Today I think of her as one of mine.

If Pam and I had let our differences in age or background or the geographical distance between us stand in the way of forming a stronger bond with one another, or if we had not listened to the prompting from the Spirit to pursue the friendship, we would've robbed ourselves of a treasure that has increased in value through the years. That is the beauty of our perceived differences—in Christ, eventually there aren't any.

On a recent trip to my hometown, I spent some time with Pam, talking about friendships, failures, and keeping our eyes on Jesus. I left her home feeling spiritually refreshed, renewed, and challenged once again. That's what iron-sharpening-iron friends do for you. And even when life gets busy, and you begin to fall out of touch, they are there for you when you extend again, or when a need arises, or when God presses on your heart to get back in touch with one another. When we open our ears to receive all our God-honoring friends have to say, their words can also be just what we need for the next time we're in a challenging situation. God can send healing words to you through a friend before a wound to your heart is even inflicted.

As I was leaving Pam's house after our lengthy discussion about friendships and failures and keeping our eyes on Jesus, she called out, "We're just here to help get each other home."

Pam's words continue to ring through my ears. We're not here for our personal affirmation or happiness, or to cross personal goals off our bucket lists. We're not here to have more friends than anyone else on our social media pages, or to get our names up in lights. We're not even here to leave a personal legacy and be remembered. We are here to live, day by day, in close connection with Jesus so we can be available for each divine appointment He sends our way to interact with others, and comfort them with the comfort we ourselves have received from God (2 Corinthians 1:3-4). We are here to help believers and unbelievers alike find their way home—because life can be difficult at times. Because people get lonely and need encouragement. Because unbelievers need to know from our example that Jesus can be trusted with their lives. And because believers need support to keep running the race of endurance, despite the struggles. Oh friend, could that be one of the reasons you and I feel lonely at times? Because we're thinking of what *we* need temporarily from others rather than what those around us need eternally?

Who can you help get home? Who could use your encouragement? As you look for who needs what you have been given, it will change your perspective and perhaps give you a renewed desire to pursue friendships.

Lord, thank You for those You have placed in my life to encourage me when I need it most. Help me to be an encourager as well.

TODAY'S CHALLENGE

Reach out to a good friend you haven't spoken with in a while. Let her know how much you appreciate her and that you want to stay in touch.

WHEN FRIENDSHIPS HURT

Faithful are the wounds of a friend.

PROVERBS 27:6

After telling me about one of her most painful struggles with a friend, Pam quoted Proverbs 27:6: "Faithful are the wounds of a friend." But then she added that Jesus has been her most faithful friend all through some of her deepest friendship wounds.

I left Pam's house thinking about the faithfulness of God in our friendships

"Thank You, God," I prayed aloud, "for friends I can spend hours with who challenge me, sharpen me, and are still waiting for me the next time I come around."

Later that afternoon, I got together with another longtime friend I rarely have a chance to see. We were excited about getting together. I spent more time with her than I felt I had available that day, and after sensing I had worn out my welcome, we hugged on the porch (just like at Pam's house), and then I went home, again thanking God for opportunities to spend hours with friends on this visit to my hometown.

Early the next morning, however, I learned that the second friend I visited with did not think our time together went well. Through a text message, she let me know I had hurt her by making her feel there wasn't enough time for her to share her heart. It hurt me that I hurt her. And I sensed the downward spiral in my thoughts.

Can't you ever get this right, Cindi? Why do you even try?

Instead of sinking into the enemy's pit of isolation and accusation where he could play on my insecurities, I took the situation to the Lord in prayer, remembered Pam's words the day earlier, and thanked God for the wound, even though it was still raw and hurting.

Within a couple hours, I was at my dad's church service with him, where I was being lifted up by other believers. It happened to be Friendship Sunday, and during the sermon that morning, I was reminded again that "faithful are the wounds of a friend." I realized God had allowed me to hear wise words from Pam on Saturday that were exactly what I would need on Sunday, as well as soothing words from Lori, another longtime friend, that same morning after church.

When we surround ourselves with God's people, He can provide one friend after another to meet us where we most need to be met in our difficulties and friendship misunderstandings. God often places friends in our lives *just* when we need them, but sometimes even *before* we need them, so their encouraging words, like Pam's a day earlier, can pour over us like honey—"sweet to the soul and healing to the bones" (Proverbs 16:24). God's timing works like that. And your friends who are surrendered to Jesus and discerning of the Holy Spirit's voice can provide soothing, healing words even before they're needed, or shortly thereafter.

Although God allows us to be wounded through some of our friends, He also allows others to step in and help heal those wounds so we grow through them. But if we stay on our island and think *I'm done with friends*, or *I'm fine on my own*, and detach ourselves from the active body of Christ, we miss the opportunity for others to minister to our hearts—and to let God refine our character through our hurts and misunderstandings.

Before I started the long drive home after church, I received another text message, this time from my neighbor, whose two-year-old daughter wanted to bring me artwork she colored before going to Sunday school.

And when I returned home later that afternoon, physically and emotionally spent, there was a tiny drawing stuck on my front door from another little neighbor—a five-year-old, who drew a picture of a smiling girl's face next to a heart.

God always knows when I'm down and need to be reminded of His love for me through a "random" act of kindness. And He knows what *you* need as well. The body of Christ is not limited to those in our local church, nor to adults, nor to friends in our hometown. Jesus has many hands and feet and hugs and little drawings for us if we will open our eyes to see and ears to hear His sweet whispers of love from those in His body whom He has surrounded us with.

Do you have wounds when it comes to friendships? We all do. But don't let yours keep you from remembering that God is faithful in spite of those wounds to help you sense *His* love for you, His forgiveness you can extend toward others, and His grace for another chance.

Lord, thank You for the wounds You allow to draw me closer and make me more like You. Help me to be a friend who soothes others' wounds because of how You've soothed mine.

TODAY'S CHALLENGE

Who could use some encouragement today from a friend who cares? Remember what your own pain feels like when you're disappointed, and extend in love to whomever God places upon your heart.

HE LOVINGLY LISTENS

Because he bends down to listen, I will
pray as long as I have breath!

PSALM 116:2 NLT

We live in a world in which people rarely listen. They may *hear* what you say, in the moment, but as my grown daughter will tell me at times, "Mom, you're not *really* listening. Other things are on your mind."

How it hurts my heart to hear that, to think that is me. My intention is to be fully in the moment with her—and with anyone who speaks to me. But as quickly as thoughts race through my mind and I am preparing what to say next, the words spoken to me are lost and replaced by my own internal words. I regrettably find myself responding, "I'm sorry. I wasn't listening carefully. Will you please say that again?"

Oh, to be one who *really* listens.

James 1:19 urges, "Everyone must be quick to hear, slow to speak, and slow to anger." We are to be *quick to hear*, rather than quick to form our thoughts of what we want to say next out of retaliation or defense (or wanting to state our opinion). The Easy-to-Read Version (ERV) translates that verse: "Always be more willing to listen than to speak. Keep control of your anger." To listen, that verse implies, is a way of controlling your anger. Hear someone out. Get the whole picture. James 1:19 in *The Message* reads, "Post this at all the intersections, dear friends: Lead with your ears, follow up with your tongue, and let anger straggle along in the rear."

My problem isn't that I respond in anger because I haven't thoroughly listened. My problem is really listening in the first place. I tend to want to move ahead to the conclusion or ending of the story, instead of enjoying the details and dialogue. Or I want to interject my thoughts before I forget what I was going to say. Or I want to verbally track with the speaker to make sure I'm processing what they're saying, but it comes across as interrupting. Yet to be quick to hear, or to focus first on hearing before speaking, is how you and I can show others we love them, just as the God who hears shows you and me that He loves us by the way He so tenderly listens.

Another variation of Psalm 116:2 tells us, "Because He has *turned His ear to me*, I will call out to Him as long as I live" (HCSB). Other versions render that verse:

- "I'll call out to him as long as I live, because he *listens closely* to me" (CEB).

- "You *paid attention* to me, and so I will pray to you as long as I live" (CEV).

- "Because he bends down to listen, I will pray as long as I have breath!" (NLT).

I love how one particular translation includes the details of God's tender response to our prayers: "He leaned down when I was in trouble and brought His ear close to me. So as long as I have breath, I will call on Him" (The Voice).

That's the beautiful way God models the art and loving act of listening—taking the time to bend down to hear what His precious child says, regardless of whether it's relevant, or mature, or the right perspective, or necessary. He listens because He's a God who bends down to hear, not missing a word and never racing ahead in His mind for what He's going to say to straighten us out or correct our thinking. First, He listens. Then, if we listen too, He lovingly speaks.

I was so moved the day I came to understand what James 1:5 says about the loving patience and listening heart of our Lord. In that verse, we're told "if any of you lacks wisdom, he should ask God, who gives to all generously and without criticizing, and it will be given to him" (HCSB).

Our God who listens won't stingily give us just a bit of what we ask for because of how much He gave us last time that we failed to use. He won't remind us of how many times we've asked and He's answered and we still can't get it right. He won't even be thinking, *It's about time you asked, and if you'd asked earlier, you could've saved yourself from a huge mess!* Nope. Scripture says He will guide us through what we need as a loving, patient Father who is so glad His daughter asked. In another version, James 1:5 reads: "If you don't know what you're doing, pray to the Father. He loves to help. You'll get his help, and won't be condescended to when you ask for it. Ask boldly, believingly, without a second thought" (MSG). Ask like a daughter confident in her loving father, who *always* takes time to listen.

Lord, thank You that You listen more intently than anyone else and You hear even the things I haven't yet said. Help me to be a listener like You, and to take time to hear what both You and others have to say.

TODAY'S CHALLENGE

Look for opportunities to *really listen* to someone today. As you do, try to hear their heart in their words, as a way of modeling how God always listens to you.

POURING OUT YOUR HEART

Trust in Him at all times, you people;
pour out your hearts before Him;
God is a refuge for us.

Psalm 62:8

Some people are *internal* processors. They run thoughts through their minds and at times find it difficult to verbally express what's on their hearts.

At times, I wish I were that way. To the contrary, I struggle with keeping it all inside. As a verbal processor, I repeat instructions aloud to make sure I understand them. And I express my thoughts verbally as a way of sorting through them. To my husband, that's exhausting at times. For me, it's essential. To hold it in is to put a stopper on my heart and I feel I will suffocate—until pent-up feelings eventually blow, like an eruption of emotion that can be overwhelming to those I love the most. In the aftermath of a gush of words, there can sometimes be regret.

But God is not threatened by my words—nor yours. And He's not irritated by our silence, either. He tells us, in His Word, to pour out our hearts before Him, and then He tells us He is a refuge, a safe place—we don't need to fear what we said or the words we withheld. He knows and can handle them all—or none at all.

And if you're one who struggles with how to verbally express how you feel, or you despair over having chosen the wrong words when you do, His Spirit will communicate with yours and express your very heart to your Heavenly Father (Romans 8:26). Psalm 62:8 says: "Trust God, my friends, and always tell him each of your concerns. God is our place of safety" (CEV).

Could you use a safe place when it comes to baring your soul? Do you need a refuge, a place to hide, when you're not ready to express how you feel? He is there for you whenever you need to process your thoughts and feelings. He is the Ultimate Listener and the Perfect Communicator. He is the Quiet Encourager and your Comforting Presence.

Remember Psalm 116:2: "Because he *bends down to listen*, I will pray as long as I have breath!" (NLT). I love how that verse indicates He will come *near* us, rather than walk away, when we have something we need to say. He will draw closer—to listen carefully—when He knows we are struggling with how to express what's on our hearts, or how to filter our words. As a father with an ear bent toward his beloved daughter, our God will listen. So, pour it out. Or keep it in, and close your eyes and reflect on being in His presence. He knows exactly what you need to say. He can hear your *unspoken* words too.

I often think David the psalmist needed to write music and lyrics so he could express his heart. And I believe he counted on God to help him find the words for what he felt so he could express those words to God and sing them back to Him. In doing so, David experienced God's strength in the midst of his weakness. I think that's why he often sang of God being his refuge and his strength. Perhaps it's why he opened Psalm 18, a description of God's physical rescue of him, with these beautiful words:

> "I love You, LORD, my strength."
> The LORD is my rock and my fortress and my savior,
> My God, my rock, in whom I take refuge (verses 1-2).

Are you struggling for the right words to express to someone today? Can you tell it to God instead, or ask Him to search your mind and thoughts and help you convey that message? Many times, when I'm at a loss for how to say something to someone at the right time and in the right way, I've asked my Heavenly Father to convey to that person what's on my heart without me having to say anything. He has an amazing way of touching someone's heart and making them "hear" what I really wanted to say to them, but never found the words to do so.

Oh, the overwhelming, astounding love of God. All His ways are perfect (Psalm 18:30). And through His help we are strengthened.

The next time you need to speak up or hold it in, praise Him with David's song for being your help with what you need to say:

> It is you who light my lamp;
> the LORD my God lightens my darkness.
> For by you I can run against a troop,
> and by my God I can leap over a wall.
> This God—his way is perfect;
> the word of the LORD proves true;
> he is a shield for all those who take refuge in
> him (Psalm 18:28-30 ESV).

"I love You, God—you make me strong. [You are] bedrock under my feet, the castle in which I live, my rescuing knight" (Psalm 18:1 MSG). Thank You for strengthening me with Your listening ear and Your interceding words.

TODAY'S CHALLENGE

Ask God to give you the words you need to say to someone, or to convey what's on your heart to that person in His way and in His time.

DAY 27

YOUR PROTECTIVE SHIELD

You, LORD, are a shield around me,
my glory, and the One who lifts my head.

PSALM 3:3

*S*ometimes we can feel alone when a comment, observation, or
insinuation leaves us feeling vulnerable or exposed.

My daughter Dana—an only child who has always been
quite independent and never "needy" of a man in her life (her mom
smiles proudly)—never feels alone until someone (who means well, of
course) asks her if she's "in a relationship yet." And after they express their
confidence that she'll one day "find a husband and be happy," she can
tend to feel singled out as inadequate or incomplete, even though she's
content with where God has her and is not striving for a relationship.

A friend who is recently divorced and knows a closeness with God
she hadn't experienced while married will suddenly feel awkward and
unprotected when someone mentions her "struggle" and expresses their
sympathy—or judgment—for her predicament.

"Don't other believers consider that we can be alone and closer to
God than when we had a man in our life?" she asked me.

And Janie, who is a young mom, feels isolated and alone when she faces—or makes—a decision concerning her toddler that other moms might criticize or at least not agree with. "As a new mom, I feel alone when I need to make an important decision for my child and there is no right or wrong answer. There isn't anyone to walk me through the different scenarios and the best options for me and my child because there are negatives on both sides. This also makes me feel inadequate because I don't feel confident in either choice."

Oh, how we need a protective shield. Something to guard our hearts from even unintentional comments that feel like arrows piercing our hearts. And oh, how our God has already provided.

"You, LORD, are a *shield* around me, my glory, the One who lifts my head high," David sang in Psalm 3:3 (NIV).

Our God is a ***shield of protection around us*** and the One who *lifts our heads high* when we would otherwise hang them low—feeling outnumbered, outclassed, outvoted, or just left out. Because He is a shield of protection around us, He enables us to hold our heads high in God-confidence.

David sang in Psalm 5:12: "You bless the righteous person, LORD, you surround him with favor as with a *shield*." God's protective shield around us is also a ***shield of favor***. Do you realize, as His child, you remain in a circle of God's favor that protects you in ways you can't imagine? In Psalm 139:5, David must've been describing God's shielding circle around him when he sang, "You have encircled me behind and in front, and placed Your hand upon me." God, as a protective enclosing shield, goes before us, moves alongside us, and guards our backs.

David again described God as a shield in Psalm 7:10 when he sang, "My *shield* is God Most High, who saves the upright in heart" (NIV). God Himself is our shield.

And in Psalm 18, David proclaimed God as a ***shield of refuge*** when he said the God who is his rock, fortress, and deliver is also his "*shield and the horn of my salvation, my stronghold*" (verses 1-2). After describing God's mighty rescue of him, David declared in verse 30: "As for God, His way is blameless; the word of the LORD is refined; He is a *shield* to *all* who take refuge in Him." And in verse 35, David lifted up his personal praise to God as his ***shield of support*** when he sang, "You protect me with your saving *shield*. You support me with your right hand. You have stooped to make me great" (NCV).

When someone says something to make us feel awkward, isolated, or alone, you and I don't have to stoop down to their level for a cutting comeback or wilt inside from a sense of awkwardness, embarrassment, or shame. God has *already* stooped for us and toward us to be our shield and protector. In the New English Translation, the end of verse 35 reads: "You give me your protective shield; your right hand supports me. Your *willingness to help* enables me to prevail."

The God of the Universe is *willing* to help us, and knowing that enables you and me to prevail, press forward, and persevere on the path He has placed us.

One morning, I highlighted in my Bible every time God was described as a shield in the book of Psalms. This description of Him occurs more than a dozen times, and this is what I learned:

- "The LORD is my strength and my shield" (Psalm 28:7).

- "He is our help and our shield" (Psalm 33:20).

- He is described as "…Lord, our shield" (Psalm 59:11).

- "The LORD God is a sun and shield" (Psalm 84:11—He's a sun that directs us and a shield that protects us!).

- "His faithfulness is a shield and wall" (Psalm 91:4).

Lord, thank You for Your shield around me. I can be among others knowing You are shielding me and loving me through any misunderstanding, insult, or offense.

TODAY'S CHALLENGE

Remember your shield of protection wherever you go, whatever you do, whatever you may hear.

DAY 28

WHAT ABOUT HER?

You have always been with me, and
all that is mine is yours.

Luke 15:31

oes jealousy ever enter your heart?

All we have to do is scroll through social media and see another post about someone's new house, new car, new man, or new *whatever,* and we can burn with jealousy, a sense of entitlement, or a state of comparison.

Where is my share? Why does she have that? I've been living far closer to God, and I don't yet have what she is bragging about. Lord, what gives?

I hate it when those thoughts bombard my mind. I desire a heart that wants only the best for others. I want to rejoice with those who rejoice and mourn with those who mourn. Don't you?

When comparison mode sneaks up in our hearts, we can eliminate it by taking another look at the story of the lost son who returned to his father (Luke 15:11-32). In that story, which we commonly refer to as the parable of the prodigal son, we see an older brother who was jealous at the attention—and *celebration*—his rebellious younger brother received upon returning home after squandering all that he had. That older brother had just finished a hard day's work in his father's field when he learned all the commotion coming from the house was a party taking place in his foolish brother's honor! He had been working hard all day while his dad was making plans to throw a party for the loser who hadn't been around in quite a long time.

Angry, the older brother refused to join the welcome-home party and found a quiet place outside to sulk. His father came to find him and pleaded with him to not have that attitude, but to join the family, friends, and servants in the celebration.

Still sulking, the offended son reminded his father of his loyalty and his unfair treatment: "Look! All these years I've been slaving for you and never disobeyed your orders. Yet you never gave me even a young goat so I could celebrate with my friends. But when this son of yours who has squandered your property with prostitutes comes home, you kill the fattened calf for him!" (verses 29-30 NIV).

In other words, "What about *me*? I've worked hard for you and never done half as many bad things as *that person* has, and you've never honored *me* like that."

Does that sound a little like you and me, at times, after seeing others get all sorts of kudos, affirmations, or blessings when they haven't lived half as well as we have? We keep waiting for our share, but it's as if God hasn't noticed we've tried to live uprightly all these years and He hasn't been blessing us for it. Perhaps we, like the older brother in the story, feel a bit resentful at God and a little less important to Him or a little left out because of someone else who is receiving His blessing at the moment.

The gracious words of the wise father to his oldest son penetrate my heart every time I start thinking my Heavenly Father has neglected me or not treated me as well as someone else.

My child, you have always been with Me, and all that is Mine is yours.

You and I *already have* all that belongs to our Heavenly Father. And just because someone else posts their blessings at a time when we might not be feeling particularly blessed doesn't mean we don't still have access to His best and aren't still heirs of all He owns. Scripture tells us, "What God has planned for people who love him is more than eyes have seen or ears have heard. It has never even entered our minds!" (1 Corinthians 2:9 CEV).

Not only does the story of the rebellious son (and the jealous one) show us a compassionate Father to whom we can always return, but it shows us the selfish perspective our hearts can hold when we forget that all our Father has is ours, and our greatest blessing is hearing His affirming words in our heart: *You have always been with Me.*

Can you follow the command in Colossians 3:2 and "set your minds on the things that are above, not on the things that are on earth"? As you do, the posts and proclamations of others won't even compare to what is awaiting you in your heavenly home. And you will be able to rejoice with those who rejoice, and weep with those who weep (Romans 12:15).

Lord, forgive me for the times I start to resent what others receive because I feel I deserved it instead. You have abundantly blessed me with Your presence and my eternal inheritance that I have— not just someday, but right now—as I live close to Your heart. Keep me focused on things above and ever remind me that all You have is mine and I am forever Yours.

TODAY'S CHALLENGE

Talk with God right now about any way that you have felt overlooked. He already knows, but He wants you to bring it to Him. Then thank Him for what He has already given you.

CONTENTMENT, NOT COMPARISON

True godliness with contentment is itself great wealth.

1 Timothy 6:6 nlt

A 24-year-old married professional told me about how social media, while it can be used for good, can also make a woman feel extremely isolated and lonely.

"It's so easy to open an app and see all the things other women are doing—their luxurious trips, perfect marriages, well-behaved kids, immaculate houses…you name it. And while these are just snippets and not a complete look into their lives, they can so easily cause us to play the comparison game and think that we are the *only* ones with a messy house or no fun weekend plans," she said.

Oh, the trap of comparison. How it can plant a seed of jealousy in our hearts—and before we know it, we are not rejoicing with those who rejoice or mourning with those who mourn. We are secretly thinking, *Why can't I have that?* And without realizing it, a seed of bitterness begins to grow in our hearts.

I know you don't want to live that way. Neither do I. God will set you free from the comparison trap when you…

- ***Remember to be thankful.*** First Thessalonians 5:18 commands us: "In everything give thanks; for this is the will of God for you in Christ Jesus." To be thanking the Lord in *all* things—even when we don't have what others have—is a tangible way of remaining in the will of God. And God's nature is to bless as we abide in His will. Remaining thankful in all things is a sign of trust. It's a sign of surrender. And it is evidence of our obedience.

- ***Rejoice in the successes and accomplishments of others.*** It's so easy to become jealous or even resentful when we see others experiencing what we want, especially when they don't appear to be living for God. But their situations are different. God sees each of our hearts and circumstances and He also sees eternally, not just temporally. Remember Jesus' words in Matthew 7:11: "If you then, who are evil, know how to give good gifts to your children, how much more will your Father who is in heaven give good things to those who ask him!" (esv). Trust that promise of His. As you rejoice with others who are joyful, God will see your mature and grateful heart.

- ***Rely on God's knowledge of what's best for you.*** Psalm 84:11 tells us, "No good thing does [God] withhold from those who walk uprightly" (esv). If you are walking uprightly and asking God for a good thing and it appears that He is still withholding, your request either isn't really good for you, or it isn't time. Trust Him with what He deems best. Just because someone else looks happy in their Instagram post doesn't mean they are. Photos don't tell the whole story and can even tell lies altogether.

- ***Recount God's faithfulness toward you.*** When we are focused on what we don't have and what we still want, we can forget how good and faithful God has already been to us. When feelings of discontent or jealousy creep into my heart, I take inventory of what I have, and instant conviction sets in. *I have so much, Lord. How can I possibly want more?* Sometimes it's a matter of whispering a simple prayer: "All I want is You, God," or "You are more than enough. Help me find my satisfaction in You." Write an encouraging text or email to someone, letting them know how thankful you are for what you have, and that may help change your perspective altogether.

- ***Return to a heart of humility.*** To compare ourselves to others is to have a heart of entitlement. *I should have what she has. I earned that; she didn't. When am I going to be blessed in that way?* The common denominator in all those complaints is the pronoun *I*. When I see things that start to shift my heart's state of contentment, I must remember that my life is not my own—I have been bought with a price, and I can give up a few things considering all that my Lord gave up for me. When you and I have Jesus, we have it all. Recognizing that helps to end the comparison game and keep jealousy at bay.

O Lord, help me to be content with You alone, and to remember to be thankful for everything I have, which is everything You have given me. On those days when I start to feel competitive or the need to compare myself to others, help me to fall back into Your arms and remember I have more than I realize.

TODAY'S CHALLENGE

The moment jealousy or comparison begins to rise in your heart, confess it to God and pray for the woman you were comparing yourself with. As we pray for others, our hearts change toward them. Take an extra step by letting that woman know how happy you are for her. It will do wonders for your heart.

A DIVINE CALLING

I wish everyone were single, just as I am.
Yet each person has a special gift from
God, of one kind or another.

1 CORINTHIANS 7:7 NLT

*T*here are some who believe that a woman's ultimate calling in life is to find a man, marry, bear children, and live happily ever after. (Or at least those first three, because every woman who marries knows that is *not* the formula for happiness.)

Although God created Eve to be Adam's helper, that did not mean it is *every* woman's calling and destiny to marry a man.

The apostle Paul said remaining single for life is a calling or a gift, and not everyone is strong enough to live that way. Let's look at the bigger context of what he said about this in 1 Corinthians 7:6-9:

> I say this as a concession, not as a command. But I wish everyone were single, just as I am. Yet each person has a

special gift from God, of one kind or another. So I say
to those who aren't married and to widows—it's better
to stay unmarried, just as I am. But if they can't control
themselves, they should go ahead and marry. It's better
to marry than to burn with lust (NLT).

Scripture is implying that both singleness and marriage are gifts. Yet
there are some who think that only marriage is a gift and sign of God's
favor, and singlehood isn't. While finding a godly man and getting married and bearing children can be callings and gifts from God, that doesn't
mean they are God's best for every woman's life. Singleness can be just
as much a calling and gift from Him.

God wants us to seek Him and His kingdom first (Matthew 6:33),
and it might be part of His plan to help you serve Him better with a
godly man by your side. But it also might not. For some, marriage and
motherhood have become cultural and often spiritual expectations of
what they believe is best for women. Yet God alone knows what is ideal
for each one of us. So, if you are living in obedience to Him and He
hasn't matched you up with a godly man (which He is more than capable of doing), He must have plans that are better suited for you. As you
walk in obedience to God, He will direct your path, and that path might
lead toward marriage with a godly man, or it might lead you toward a life
of being single. If God's path for you is to remain single (indefinitely, or
after being widowed or divorced), it will be a far better life for you than
marriage or remarriage would have brought.

My daughter, Dana, is now in her early 30s, single, loves God, and
loves the career path He has given her. In her proud mom's opinion, she
is a role model for contentment in where God has called her.

Dana recently told me, "I know, without a doubt, God would rather see me content and single and living a life that pleases Him, than in a marriage where I'm unhappy, or in which I found a man who will support me so I'll *eventually* be happy."

Dana and many women her age have seen friends marry because they were "in love" at the time, or sought the financial stability of a husband, or were "in the stage of life where it makes sense to marry," only to find themselves no more content than when they were single.

For decades, I've seen women stay in a miserable dating relationship with a man they weren't married to, rather than leave him and trust God for a better life *without* a man. I've seen women marry men who didn't treat them well because they feared never marrying at all. And I've seen women go through "serial marriages"—one husband after another—in search of the man they believe will finally make them feel happy, loved, and fulfilled.

Remember, God brings reward to those who trust Him, not to those who try to find a way to make marriage happen no matter what it looks like.

Perhaps you love God with all your heart and are obedient to Him, and still have not found a God-honoring man worthy of your hand in marriage. Don't think for a minute, dear friend, that God will not honor your high standards of wanting His best for you. Perhaps following God's path for you will lead you to an opportunity that is beyond anything you have imagined thus far—an opportunity to serve others or do things you couldn't do if you were married. And that might even include loving and caring for far more children than if you were to marry and bear your own!

Our ultimate calling is to *The Man*—Jesus—not *a* man. As you walk the path God lays before you, whether there's a husband on that path or not, you will experience His joy.

Lord, help me to be content with what You've given me, not wishing for a moment that I have what someone else has.

TODAY'S CHALLENGE

Praise God, throughout your day, that He knows what's best for your life at this moment—and always.

WHY DOES GOD SEEM DISTANT?

*And let us not neglect our meeting together, as some
people do, but encourage one another, especially
now that the day of his return is drawing near.*

HEBREWS 10:25 NLT

*A*re there days when you feel lonely and you wonder why? Isn't
God supposed to always be with you? Didn't He say He would
never leave you? (Hebrews 13:5). So why do you still *feel* lonely?
Often, we are tempted to say, "God's not speaking to me. He's become
distant." But in reality, we are the ones who have stopped talking, stopped
listening, or moved further away from Him.

God promises in His Word that nothing can separate us from His
love (Romans 8:38-39), so if you feel like God has become distant, perhaps it's a result of one of these scenarios:

You might not be following Him closely. When we are not living
in obedience as followers of Jesus, the abundant life Jesus promised us
in John 15:4-5—which tells us that when we abide in Him, we bear

fruit—is not ours, and this can result in feeling anxious, uncertain, and lonely. Through a lack of obedience to God or misplaced priorities, we can hold back the blessings He has for those who fully surrender to Him. It's possible to possess a head knowledge of God (we know what we're supposed to do and not to do), without engaging our hearts and loving Him with all that we are. That's when we become stuck between the now and the not yet. We live in the now of the difficulties of life on our own and have not yet experienced the joys and blessings of a life fully surrendered to Him. The more you pursue a closer relationship with God, the more you will experience the fulfillment you seek.[6]

> The more you pursue a closer relationship with God, the more you will experience the fulfillment you seek.

You might be worrying and not clinging to His Word. Mark 4:19 tells us the *worries of this world* choke the Word's fruitfulness in our lives. If we feel as though God is not talking to us through His Word, it may be because we are worriers, and our worrisome thoughts and anxieties are drowning out God's voice. Don't underestimate the importance of being in God's Word regularly so you can grow closer to Jesus and keep away from sin (worry is just one sin among many). Psalm 119:9 asks: "How can a [person] keep his way pure? By keeping it according to Your word." To live in close relationship with God is to embrace Jesus and His Word because Jesus is defined in John 1:1 *as* the Word. To accept Him is to accept His Word. To love Him is to love His Word. To obey Him and abide in (or dwell closely with) Him is to obey and abide in His Word. God's Word is for us today just as much as Jesus is for us today. We can't separate the two or claim we want Jesus, but His

Word is no longer relevant. Abiding in His Word is not optional for the follower of Christ, it's *essential*.

You might be avoiding other believers. Ignoring God's commands in His Word, harboring sin, or avoiding community with other Christ-followers can also lead to feelings of loneliness. In Psalm 25, David asked God to turn to him and be gracious to him because he was *lonely and afflicted*. David prayed, "Relieve the troubles of my heart and free me from my anguish. Look on my affliction and my distress and take away all my sins" (verses 16-18 NIV).

David acknowledged a direct correlation between sin in his life and the loneliness he experienced—likely from a separation from God's presence and God's people. (While sin itself doesn't separate us from God's presence, it will hinder the closeness of our relationship with Him, and we often voluntarily separate ourselves from God's people when we're in sin.) David ended his song with these words: "May integrity and uprightness protect me, because *my hope, LORD, is in you*" (verse 21 NIV).

David knew that the key to personal fulfillment and even God's protection was that he maintain integrity and uprightness and keep his hope firmly in the Lord. Integrity and uprightness can put us in a place where we experience less loneliness. And we can live with integrity when we embrace God's Word and welcome the fellowship and accountability of God's people.

Do you need to set your heart on growing in your love relationship with God? Do you need to get into His Word so you will know Him more fully? Or do you need to connect with a local church and become more closely connected with other believers?

God is waiting for you to leave behind your loneliness and experience His presence—and His people—once again.

Lord, I realize You are not the One who distances Yourself. Help me to get back into Your Word and into the places where Your people gather.

TODAY'S CHALLENGE

Ask God to make it very clear what you need to do to put yourself in the position where you are more closely connected with Him and His people.

BEAUTY, NOT THE BEAST

*I have been crucified with Christ; and it is no longer
I who live, but Christ lives in me; and the life which
I now live in the flesh I live by faith in the Son of
God, who loved me and gave Himself up for me.*

GALATIANS 2:20

How I long for my life to exhibit the beauty of Christ, not the beast of self. How I want the sweet perfume of God's fragrance to emanate from me, not the sour stench of pride and selfish ambition.

In the classic tale *Beauty and the Beast*, the monster is selfish, self-serving, and looks out not for the interest of others, but only for himself. The beast, which is what I become apart from Christ, is

- lacking in compassion
- brash and rude
- focused on self-preservation, not self-sacrifice
- indulgent, impulsive, excessive

- loud and calls attention to self

- quick to anger

- critical, judgmental, unloving

The beast knows nothing of Calvary love, of irresistible grace, of the tender mercies of Christ.

But Jesus is true beauty. He is loving, caring, compassionate, a humble servant. He is

- full of compassion

- gentle and courteous

- a servant of others

- humble, thoughtful, generous

- quiet and gives glory to the Father

- slow to anger and abounding in lovingkindness

- kind, gracious, forgiving

Beauty knows everything of sacrificial love. He became a sacrifice for you and me. He became Love Incarnate.

Philippians 2:3-4 tells us to "do nothing from selfishness or empty conceit, but with humility consider one another as more important than yourselves; do not merely look out for your own personal interests, but also for the interests of others." And the next four verses instruct us Whom we should model our behavior and attitude after:

> Have this attitude in yourselves which was also in Christ Jesus, who, as He already existed in the form of God, did not consider equality with God something to

be grasped, but emptied Himself by taking the form of a bond-servant and being born in the likeness of men. And being found in appearance as a man, He humbled Himself by becoming obedient to the point of death: death on a cross (verses 5-8).

How can you and I die to self (the beast) and live to Christ, preferring His ways over our own? It happens with one small choice after another to place others before ourselves. As we set our minds on dying to our own desires, the life we live will be His, and it will emanate with beauty.

The apostle Paul's proclamation in Galatians 2:20 now takes on a whole new light as instructions for how you and I can live as beauty, and not the beast:

My old self has been crucified with Christ. It is no longer I who live, but Christ lives in me. So I live in this earthly body by trusting in the Son of God, who loved me and gave himself for me (NLT).

In *The Message*, that verse reads:

Indeed, I have been crucified with Christ. My ego is no longer central. It is no longer important that I appear righteous before [others] or have [their] good opinion, and I am no longer driven to impress God. Christ lives in me. The life you see me living is not "mine," but it is lived by faith in the Son of God, who loved me and gave himself for me.

What a confirmation that our beastly identity has been *crucified with Christ*; it no longer exists. Christ's beautiful life has taken over.

You and I have been *crucified* with Christ.

"Kill the beast!" becomes our battle cry.

The beast in us consumes all things, distorts all things, destroys all things, devours all things. But *love*—His love—"bears all things, believes all things, hopes all things, endures all things" (1 Corinthians 13:7 ESV).

Christlike love never fails.

Which do you want your life to resemble? You and I can so easily become the beast and look out for our own interests, parade our glories before others, fail to notice those around us who are hurting. Or, we can instead be the sweet aroma of a rose to those around us, bringing beauty to all we encounter when we carry the presence of God with us—the humility, gentleness, and self-sacrificial attitude that Christ displayed—into our friendships and family relationships. How can that Christlike attitude and behavior not transform another person who is also acting more like the beast than the beauty of our Lord?

O Lord, kill the beast in me. Soften my rough edges. Break my heart with what breaks Yours so Your love may flow out of me to others and impact their lives for Your glory.

TODAY'S CHALLENGE

In a journal or in the space below, list tangible ways you can be focused on those around you, rather than yourself. It is, after all, part of your new nature in Christ.

WHEN DEATH STINGS

*Precious in the sight of the LORD is
the death of His godly ones.*

PSALM 116:15

The loss of a loved one can be one of the loneliest feelings we experience. To have someone close to you—a friend, a sibling, a parent, a husband, a child—ripped away from you suddenly, or even gradually, can tear at the insides of your heart.

Don't ever feel ashamed for grieving the loss of someone you love, thinking it shows a lack of faith in your hope of heaven. Don't ever let someone tell you that it's time to stop grieving and you should be over it by now.

While you may have been told death is a natural part of life, it most certainly is not. You and I were created to live forever in paradise with our Creator God, enjoying the pleasure of His presence and the perfect world He placed us in. Yet the ravages of sin destroyed that. And now death is sweet only because it is the transition through which we meet our Savior if we are indeed His.

You and I were never meant to experience death and the pain of separation from those who leave this earth before us. Yet sin from Adam and Eve, our ancestors, led to spiritual death (separation from God) and physical death (the ultimate end of a body affected by sin). Thus, death is *not* a natural, God-intended part of life. But *grieving* death is. Even for a believer.

My prayer for my Aunt Alice, as she was slowly ending her life at nearly 92 years old, was that God would take her peacefully—transition her from her earthly home to her heavenly home in a beautiful moment. And that, He did. As my cousin, Tami, played the worship song "I Can Only Imagine" and held her mother's hand and stroked her forehead, her mom passed peacefully into the arms of her Savior. Scripture says the death of the Lord's godly ones is precious in His sight. How precious was Aunt Alice's homegoing. And while Tami grieves the loss of her mom by missing her presence and realizing she no longer has a living parent on this earth, she rejoices that her mom is now completely restored—her memory, her hearing, her health, her vitality. Alice is now completely whole and fulfilled as she was created to be.

The morning I learned of Aunt Alice's passing was the moment I realized she was finally experiencing "fullness of joy" in God's presence and "eternal pleasures at [His] right hand" (Psalm 16:11). She was reunited not only with her precious Savior, but with her servant-husband of 65 years (who died less than a year before she did), and with her two oldest sons, who entered heaven years earlier.

While the ache of separation remains for all of us who lose a loved one, the thought of heaven brings hope that lightens the load of grieving. Oh, how wonderful heaven will be! And as we keep our focus there on what is to come when we will be in the presence of Jesus, we can comfort our grieving hearts. Yes, we continue to miss the presence of our loved ones here, but oh, the peace that comes from knowing they are experiencing inexpressible joy and we will one day join them.

Upon processing Alice's death, and Tami and her brother's care for both their parents in their last years of life, I was struck with the longing to live wisely and well during these last years of my own parents' lives—to take every opportunity to show love, say what needs to be said, take every chance to love them like there's no tomorrow. Because there might not be. (And I had no idea Tami's encouragement to me was so needed, as I would lose my own mom within a year of her losing hers.)

Upon hearing of *anyone's* death, and contemplating my own one day, I am reminded that life is short, people's souls last forever in the presence of God or in separation from Him, and that everything I do, every word I say, can have eternal consequences. Therefore, I must remember to number my days and make every effort to live wisely and well (Psalm 90:12). A life well-lived means no regrets, no missed opportunities to show God's love, no grace-filled words left unsaid.

Whom have you lost recently? Or years ago? Does the loss still sting? It always will, my precious friend. And know that you are not alone. God understands your sadness and pain. And let His peace surround you and bring you comfort as you realize that your own death one day will be a sweet transition into the loving arms of your Savior and a reunion with His children who have passed on before you. Oh, how sweet, how *lovely* heaven will be!

Lord, set my heart on things above (Colossians 3:1-2)—on heaven, where there is no pain or suffering, and where complete restoration exists. Comfort my heart with the hope that You have a glorious future prepared for those who love You.

TODAY'S CHALLENGE

Reach out to someone today who has lost a loved one. Doing so will remind you—and that friend—they are not alone.

WHEN GRIEF LINGERS

*Thank God! He gives us victory over sin and
death through our Lord Jesus Christ.*

1 Corinthians 15:57 nlt

Hearing of Aunt Alice's sweet transition to heaven encouraged me that I would be able to get through my own parents' deaths when the time came. I was determined to treat life as fragile, and reach out to my parents often as they might have less time than I thought. Yet it was still a shock to see my mom pass so quickly and unexpectedly.

I say quick because the doctor predicted she had less than six months to live when she actually had two. Her death was unexpected because she seemed fine one day, took a drastic turn the next, and was gone within a week. It was traumatic to watch her body gradually shut down over a few days, yet also precious to be able to hold her hand and pray with her as she departed and went into the arms of her Savior.

When you and I anticipate the death of a parent or loved one, we may tell ourselves it will be okay because "they've lived a long life" if in fact they did. Or we can try to prepare ourselves for the loss by saying, "Everyone has to die at some point," and anticipating we will be fine because "they'll be in a better place." But when that moment comes (whether in person or being informed by phone), or you hear the hospital heart-rate monitor go from a steady beeping to a drawn-out buzz, or when you see their chest heave with difficulty for the very last time and they cease to breathe again, the sudden stop and lingering stillness of that life—and for a moment, of yours—can be stifling.

Scripture asks, "O death, where is your sting?" (1 Corinthians 15:55 ESV). It's still there, my friend, in the grief of the loss of someone you love. In the knowing that you will not hear their voice or feel their touch, or see life in their eyes again this side of heaven. In the devastation that the curse of death and disease has brought to this life and all we know. But within that sting that I'm told will eventually fade to a small, stabbing pain every now and then when you remember your loved one's life, there is *still hope*. There is hope that, in a saving relationship with Jesus, there is life beyond the heart that no longer beats here. There is happiness beyond what you can imagine right now. There is comfort, joy, peace, and no more pain for your loved one in Christ, who may have experienced much pain and difficulty and effort to even breathe before passing from this earth.

First Corinthians 15:54-57 assures us that when our dying bodies have been transformed into bodies that will never die, this scripture will be fulfilled:

> "Death is swallowed up in victory.
> O death, where is your victory?
>   O death, where is your sting?"

> For sin is the sting that results in death, and the law gives
> sin its power. But thank God! He gives us victory over sin
> and death through our Lord Jesus Christ (NLT).

Scripture makes it clear that if you and the loved ones you have lost are in Christ Jesus, there is a grand reunion that awaits you when your Savior calls you home. That is the eternal hope that eases the temporary sting. That is the saving power of Christ's resurrection that can't keep anyone in the grave. That is the abundant joy you can one day experience when Christ makes all things new, rights every wrong, heals every disease, and raises the redeemed to life.

If you aren't feeling that joy just yet, don't despair. Sometimes our hearts and minds can't transition to thoughts of heaven as instantaneously as the souls who are in Christ can arrive there. Scripture says that to be absent from the body is to be present with the Lord (2 Corinthians 5:8). But trauma from watching a loved one die, or dealing with the loss of their presence, can sometimes delay or dampen the feelings of joy that come from knowing they're with the Lord. Grief still stings while we remain in the place where all wrongs have not yet been made right. In the place where all disease has not yet been healed. In the place where we still experience pain and regret. Yet your glorious home awaits. And so does your Savior, with open arms to comfort you when you need to be assured that He is familiar with every memory, every hurt, every unhealed wound, every regret. He has seen every tear, even those that haven't yet fallen. He is intimately acquainted with all your ways (Psalm 139:3), and His comfort and peace are available to you at every moment.

Fall into His arms, dear one, as you embrace the pain of losing someone you love. He understands, and He will help you get to that place where heaven—and not the loss of their life here on Earth—will fill your thoughts (Colossians 3:2-3).

Lord, thank You that life and death are in Your hands and You can be trusted with both. Help me to focus on Your promise of peace and comfort, rather than the sting of grief.

TODAY'S CHALLENGE

Read Colossians 3:2-3 and let only heaven fill your thoughts.

PART III

CONNECTING WITH YOUR PURPOSE

YOU MATTER

When I consider Your heavens, the work of Your fingers,
the moon and the stars, which You have set in place;
what is man that You think of him,
and a son of man that You are concerned about him?

PSALM 8:3-4

When you hear someone's bio on a podcast or read their list of accomplishments online, do you start to think, *What have I even done with my life? How can I ever achieve something like that?*

Or maybe you've scrolled through social media profiles and looked at the number of likes, follows, or hits someone else has and you feel like you lag pretty far behind.

God is the supreme Being who has accomplished more than anyone ever will, and yet we read in His Word that He has precious thoughts of us.

In contemplating the vast universe and its multitude of galaxies, why would you and I matter in the scope of eternity? Considering the number of people in this world with far greater accomplishments than us, who are you and me to matter at all to God?

Why would He know each of us by name (Isaiah 45:3), and count the number of hairs on our heads (Luke 12:7), and collect each of our tears in a bottle (Psalm 56:8)? Who are we that He would take the time to ordain for us the number of our days before any of them came to be (Psalm 139:16)?

You and I ask those questions because we see our failures, our inadequacies, the aspects of ourselves that we wish were different. We harbor our regrets, try to hide our flaws, and long to be truly known, yet could never believe anyone who really knew us could ever still love us.

Yet our God sees it all and still chooses to love us immensely. *Why?*

The prophet Job asked that question too: "What are mortals anyway, that you bother with them, that you even give them the time of day? That you check up on them every morning, looking in on them to see how they're doing?" (Job 7:17-18 msg).

God knew we would experience feelings of insignificance and inadequacy—even self-loathing at times, wondering how anyone could find us worthy of love or acceptance. So, He breathed certain words to writers who, through the ages, released them from their quills onto the parchments of Scripture. Affirming words like these:

- "Can a mother forget her nursing child? Can she feel no love for the child she has borne? But even if that were possible, I would not forget you!" (Isaiah 49:15 nlt).

- "How precious are your thoughts about me, O God. They cannot be numbered!" (Psalm 139:17 nlt).

- "Are not five sparrows sold for two pennies? And not one of them is forgotten before God…Fear not; you are of more value than many sparrows" (Luke 12:6-7 esv).

- "See how great a love the Father has given us, that we would be called children of God; and in fact we are" (1 John 3:1).

- "In Him we have redemption through His blood, the forgiveness of our wrongdoings, according to the riches of His grace which He lavished on us. In all wisdom and insight He made known to us the mystery of His will, according to His good pleasure" (Ephesians 1:7-9).

- "You did not choose Me but I chose you" (John 15:16).

- "No longer do I call you slaves, for the slave does not know what his master is doing; but I have called you friends" (John 15:15).

Jesus, God in the flesh, calls *you* His *friend*! Think about that. Not just His creation. Not just His servant. Not even an acquaintance. Certainly, not His mistake or embarrassment. His *friend*.

When we stop focusing on ourselves—our failures, inadequacies, what we look like, how much we weigh, and where we fall short in comparison to others—and fix our eyes on the One who created us and lavished His love on us by sending His Son to die in our place so we could spend eternity with Him, we get a glimpse into just how BIG He is, and just how MUCH He loves *us*.

It isn't about who you are and what you can or cannot do. It's about the One who has chosen you, regardless of what you've done or ever will do.

Stop wondering if you're good enough and spend the rest of your days being convinced *He is more than enough*, and He has set His love on *you*. How can that not change how you live?

Thank You, God, for lavishing Your unconditional love on me. Thank You that as big as You are, as powerful as You are, as huge as Your responsibilities are in governing the universe and countless cosmos, You still know the tiny details of my life and You care about me more than I can imagine. Thank You that, because of the worthiness of what Your Son accomplished on the cross for me, You now see me as worth saving. Help me to walk on this planet differently because I know I am much loved.

TODAY'S CHALLENGE

Think of at least one thing you are thankful for when it comes to how uniquely God made you, and praise Him for that throughout the day.

OUR INEVITABLE SEARCH FOR PURPOSE

You are the light of the world. A city set on a hill
cannot be hidden…Let your light shine before
men in such a way that they may see your good
works, and glorify your Father who is in heaven.

MATTHEW 5:14, 16 NASB 1995

M y daughter Dana has many times heard me share her story of being hospitalized at 18 months old for a sudden drop in her blood platelet level, which resulted in unexplained bruising all over her body. After seeing the best blood specialist in the country, who administered a bone marrow test to determine whether she had cancer or leukemia, she experienced a rare and immediate recovery of what her pediatrician believed was an acute case of ITP.*

---

* ITP is an autoimmune condition in which one's immune system attacks and destroys its own cells by destroying healthy platelets in the spleen and liver. It also limits the production of new platelets in one's bone marrow. For more on this, see https://www.understandingitp.com/.

Knowing her medical history—along with learning that her mom and dad were unable to conceive a second child—convinced Dana at a young age that she is a miracle child a couple times over, and God must have a specific purpose and unique calling on her life. That awareness has instilled in her a God-confidence and propelled her to dream big dreams, pursue the impossible, and ask God for the unachievable. As a result, she has *never* struggled with identity issues about who she is or why she's here.

When you and I, too, realize the significance of our existence, and Who it is who has ordained every move of our lives, that understanding can convince us that we're here for a reason and it can open our eyes to discovering—and embracing—what that purpose is.

Now, I certainly wouldn't wish a health scare on a baby or secondary infertility on a set of parents for their children to realize they are here for a reason, and they have a unique calling. And you and I shouldn't have to experience a brush with death or overcome insurmountable odds to be convinced we are valuable and uniquely designed for God's purposes. The Bible has already given us ample reason to marvel at our worth in the eyes of our Creator and Sustainer, and to constantly dream of, wonder about, and imagine the plans He has for us.

Today, Dana instills creativity and imagination in children and young adults in her career job that daily brings her joy.

But when she was laid off for more than a year during the COVID pandemic, and at one point believed she had lost that job forever, she began to question her identity and her purpose.

"When I was laid off, I felt like I had no purpose because I no longer had the job that brought me a sense of purpose, joy, and fulfillment," Dana told me months later. "If I've ever felt alone in my life, that was it—when I didn't believe I had a purpose or something to look forward to. I am very good at being creative, helping people, driving things forward, and bringing others joy, so when I didn't have that connected to my job, I felt alone."

And yet, Dana also recalls that the period of uncertainty—when she felt her career and purpose were hanging in the balance—is also what God used to draw her closer to Himself.

As she focused on trusting God and placing her self-worth in His hands, He brought her opportunities to let her talents shine by working with children in a local youth theater—teaching voice lessons to kids who were unsure of who they were and whether they were loved, and helping them hone their abilities and build their confidence. By using her talents to shine, she helped children discover and display their talents as well. And then, rather unexpectedly, God handed back to her the job she loved—only better. She was promoted to full time, then given a management position over her entire department several months later. She now trains facilitators and develops content for educational programs while compassionately listening to others who aren't feeling heard, and, in her mother's opinion, is a "city set on a hill" shining Jesus' light daily in a secular entertainment company.

Look at the abilities you've been given, the unique circumstances in which you've been raised, your life experiences. Look at your wounds and what they've taught you or how they've helped you become more empathetic, and look at where God has placed you. You, too, can be a city set on a hill shining Jesus' light to others.

What's your purpose? Shine your light for Him in whatever opportunities He gives you. And you can do that even if, at this point, that light is simply a recognition that you were created with a purpose and you were lavished with love so you can be all your Creator God designed you to be.

Lord, thank You for entrusting me with the privilege of being a representative of Yours wherever I am. Help me to let Your light shine through me.

TODAY'S CHALLENGE

Ask God to open your eyes today to opportunities to shine His light.

ARE YOU DOING ENOUGH?

Stop striving and know that I am God.

PSALM 46:10

D o you ever wonder if you're *doing* enough for God?

We live in a culture that applauds activity. Where busyness is the badge of success. Where multitasking in the church is what appears to others—and ourselves—as ultra-spiritual. In contrast, while a relationship with the Living God produces a desire to obey Him and serve Him, that service results in joy and rest, not perpetual stress!

God would rather have us spend time *with* Him than do a bunch of things *for* Him. I see that in Jesus' response to a man who asked Him about the greatest of all the commandments. Jesus' answer was, "Love the Lord your God with all your heart and with all your soul and with all your mind. This is the great and first commandment. And a second is like it: You shall love your neighbor as yourself" (Matthew 22:37-39 ESV).

God is focused on relationship. Primarily, ours with Him, and then others. You and I tend to be focused on activity. He is the One who tells us to "be still" (Psalm 46:10) and to come to Him and rest (Matthew 11:28). We are the ones who are striving to do more.

As you and I spend time cultivating our love relationship with God, we will know how to serve others and how to be able to discern His gentle voice on our hearts, saying, *This is what I have for you*, or *Step in and help her with that*. But it will never be at the expense of overlooking our primary responsibilities, nor will it cause us to feel overextended.

Jesus, after all, told His closest followers during the height of His popularity, "Come with me by yourselves to a quiet place and get some rest" (Mark 6:31 NIV). He didn't say, "Let's try to cover even *more* territory today by working even harder!"

> Never underestimate the power of simply living among and working alongside nonbelievers as a committed follower of Jesus.

Whether you are a student with a full load of classes, working a demanding full-time job, juggling children at home and earning an income, or simply a woman who has her hands full (and who doesn't these days?), let me encourage you to quiet your heart and focus on your love for the Lord. As you sit at His feet, He will eventually call you to get up and serve Him in His way and His timing. But if you aren't taking time to be still, open His Word, and listen for His voice and direction, how can you possibly know how and where to serve? As you grow in your love relationship with God, you will learn how to discern the difference between His loving voice and the voice of your own guilt.

Listen for where God is calling you to serve, and go where He leads. Too many times, we find ourselves overscheduled, overwhelmed, and spiritually undernourished because we jump in to serve somewhere without asking God if that is what He wants of us.

While you and I are to exercise our spiritual gifts to uplift and encourage other believers (and that implies connection with a local church), that doesn't mean serving God occurs only on Sundays or within a church building. *Ministry happens anywhere you are salt and light, and wherever Christ is glorified through you.* Your greatest ministry in this season of life may be to support your husband, or guide your child spiritually, or be an encouraging voice in your workplace. Never underestimate the power of simply living among and working alongside nonbelievers as a committed follower of Jesus.

"Whatever you do, do it enthusiastically, as something done for the Lord and not for [people]" (Colossians 3:23 HCSB).

Our Lord did enough to secure God's forgiveness and acceptance of us when He gave His perfect life in exchange for ours as a penalty for our sin. Our service, in light of what Christ did for us on the cross, is to show our love and obedience to Him. It's not to earn His love. It's our way of showing Him evidence of ours. It's a way of saying, "I've been freed from the yoke of sin and I have a new master now...the Lord Jesus. Everything I do, I do for Him." Serving Him from that mindset brings joy, not stress.

Serve Him, dear sister, out of inspiration, not obligation, and you may find that instead of feeling guilt for not doing enough, you are feeling privileged to do the little that you can.

Lord, may I serve You today out of love and gratitude for what You have already done for me. When I begin to think I should be doing more, clarify whether that's Your whisper or my own sense of obligation or guilt feelings. And make it clear when You simply want me to rest in You.

TODAY'S CHALLENGE

Commit to the Lord whatever you do today, out of your love for Him. That's the kind of service He wants from you.

ARE YOU WILLING?

When they had rowed about three or four miles,
they saw Jesus approaching the boat, walking on
the water; and they were frightened. But he said
to them, "It is I; don't be afraid." Then they were
willing to take him into the boat, and immediately
the boat reached the shore where they were heading.

JOHN 6:19-21 NIV

I often wonder what would have happened if Jesus' followers hadn't been willing to take Him into the boat with them that night. What if they were too fearful of what they didn't understand? Jesus was walking on the water—that just doesn't happen. He could have been a ghost or a figment of their imagination. What if, out of fear or hesitation, they were too determined to work their own plan instead of letting Jesus into the boat to solve their problem? Would they have worn themselves out rowing aimlessly all night? Would they have finally, hours later, said, "Okay, we give up. Please come help us!" and regretted not saying it earlier?

Yet even though they didn't recognize Him at first—because He was showing them a side of Himself they'd never seen before (a water-walker!)—they knew His voice. They had also seen Him turn water into wine, heal the sick and lame, and even raise the dead to life. They obeyed His command—and heeded His assurance to them—to not be afraid. They instinctively knew that if He was in the boat *with them*, they would be okay and they would get to where they needed to go.

> The One who *walked* on the water, the One who *parted* the waters, the One who *provides* living water, and the One who *transformed* water into wine—can certainly calm the waters that are rocking your boat and keeping you from getting to where He wants you to be.

Once they were willing to take Jesus in—a surrender of their pride and insistence on working the problem their way, and an acknowledgment they truly needed help—they *immediately* got to the place they were heading.

You and I sometimes row against the wind. We fight the current. We battle obstacles, fear, and distractions, insisting on getting to our destination in our timing. Sometimes we even tread water or drift aimlessly out to sea because we are determined to work our plan our way, or we are afraid of what we don't understand when it comes to how Jesus will help us. We are so determined to get to a certain place in our way and our timing (and sometimes fearful of what Jesus might ask of us if we let Him in a little further), that we fail to see the One who walks on water out in front of us, the One who is fully capable of helping calm our seas and getting us where we need to go.

Are you willing to let Jesus into your boat—in His way—so He can immediately get you to where you're heading or reroute you to where you're really supposed to be?

The One who *walked* on the water, the One who *parted* the waters, the One who *provides* living water, and the One who *transformed* water into wine—can certainly calm the waters that are rocking your boat and keeping you from getting to where He wants you to be. He can walk on top of your waters, part them to clear the way, provide all you need in Him, and transform your obstacles into opportunities if you will trust Him—if you are willing to let Him into your boat and navigate for you.

Trust the Lord of the waters…He can calm the storm in you just as He calms the seas.

Trust Him in the transitions…as you're navigating new waters.

Trust Him in the unknown…as you're heading to uncharted territory. He knows exactly how to get you to where you are heading, or to where He would rather have you be.

Lord Jesus, You can do anything, so why do I hesitate to invite You into my boat from the start of the journey? Do I think I can get anywhere without You knowing? And do I possibly think I can arrive somewhere successfully if You are not steering my boat? Forgive me for the times I try to do things on my own, thinking You don't have the time or desire to help. I give You the helm. And I trust Your direction.

TODAY'S CHALLENGE

Surrender your course to Him. No matter what it looks like, He loves you and can get you to the best place possible, regardless of any storm that may be on the horizon. If it will help you truly hand Him the helm, write out a prayer of surrender to Him in the space below.

PRAISING IN THE MIDDLE OF PAIN

The LORD gave me what I had,
and the LORD has taken it away.
Praise the name of the LORD!

JOB 1:21 NLT

Can you imagine praising God, as Job did, after unimaginable loss? The story of Job in the Bible is not a parable or a fable. Job was a real man, husband, father, and farmer. In fact, he was a present-day millionaire, in a sense. The Bible says he was the "greatest" (richest) man in the East. Then everything he had—and I mean *everything*—was gone in a day.

In spite of the horrible shock of suddenly losing everything—his livestock, his livelihood, his investments, and all ten of his children—Job's response was to worship his Creator, the One who had allowed him to lose it all. In a humble, God-honoring statement that truly defined this man's character, Job responded not with questions, complaints, nor curses, but with praise:

Naked I came from my mother's womb,
and naked I shall return there.
The LORD gave and the LORD has taken away.
Blessed be the name of the LORD (verses 20-21).

How could Job have responded that way?

I imagine you and I would react quite differently after losing just half as much as Job did.

"God, *why*?"

"God, I've served You and yet *You* let this happen."

"God, are You even *there* anymore?"

Experiencing loss upon loss can have that kind of effect on us. It can make us question everything we ever knew about God.

Yet Job could praise God in his pain because, in his wisdom, he realized the one thing that mattered most to him—his God—was still with him. Job realized God was still there, God was still good, and God was still worthy of his praise. Job saw God as his greatest possession.

Job's response, however, wasn't quite as stellar when he lost his health. When his livelihood and loved ones were taken from him, the emotional pain gave way to praise. But when his body became wracked with pain, confusion, and disillusionment, his responses became more like yours and mine would be. That is when Job began to raise questions. That is when Job's friends began to offer opinions on why God was allowing his suffering. That is when Job met his darkest, most painful time—in the confusion of not understanding why God wasn't letting up.

And then we arrive at the most beautiful description in all of Scripture of Who our Creator is and all that He is capable of. In chapters 38–41, God takes our breath away when He answers Job out of his "storm"—the biggest storm God knew any man or woman would ever have to endure.

And God's big reveal? His all-coveted answer to the question *why*? It didn't come. When God finally spoke, He didn't solve the age-old mystery of why bad things happen to good people. Rather, He began with, "Why do you talk so much when you know so little?" (Job 38:2 CEV). God was, in a sense, saying, "Who are *you*, Job, to question *Me*?"

And for four long chapters, God doesn't shine a penlight of understanding on Job's circumstances, but rather, projects a spotlight on who the God of the Universe really is and all that He's capable of.

After God's discourse, Job is the one who is silent. After hearing God's description of how He rules and sustains all creation, Job is speechless. (Read God's discourse in Job 38–41 and you will be speechless too!)

The only words Job can finally utter are a declaration that God is God and Job is not: "I know that You can do all things, and that no purpose of Yours can be thwarted," Job responded to the Almighty (42:2 NASB 1995).

Do you hear his humility? Do you sense his surrender? Now listen for Job's song—the true reward for his suffering: "My ears had heard of you but now my eyes have *seen* you" (verse 5 NIV).

Oh, to know God in a way that we have "seen" Him with our spiritual eyes…understanding how great and majestic He is and yet knowing that, in spite of all He allows or prevents, He still loves us beyond reason.

What is God allowing you to go through so that you don't merely know *about* Him in your head, but truly know Him in your heart? What is He doing so you aren't merely one who has *heard* of God, but you've had the privilege of *seeing* Him by faith?

Instead of assuming or concluding your pain is your punishment from the hand of God and thinking He no longer loves you, consider that what you are going through may be God's hand extending to you an opportunity to know Him in a way you never have before. Perhaps He is inviting you to walk closer to Him than you ever thought was possible.

Lord, Your works are wondrous, Your love is beyond reason, and Your majesty is worthy of praise. You truly are the One whose breath sends the ice, who loads the clouds with moisture, and who controls the storm (Job 37:10-11, 15). In spite of all that I still want, all that I am enduring, all that I wish would change, I choose to say, "Blessed be the name of the LORD."

TODAY'S CHALLENGE

Practice surrender by telling God how much you love Him in spite of what hurts right now.

WHERE HOPE LIES

Though He slay me, I will hope in Him.
JOB 13:15

I once read that a person can live without food, shelter, water, or love. But the one thing a person cannot live without is hope.

What is the hope that keeps you alive?

Is it a hope for your future? A hope to one day have a family? A hope for authentic love? Maybe it's a hope for purpose—to know what you're living for.

What if I were to tell you that the key to your future, your discovery of authentic love, and your sense of fulfillment and purpose is found in making the Lord your hope?

Imagine losing everything and feeling there was no hope at all. We just looked at Job's incredible response to God after losing all he had materially, financially, and emotionally. Today, look with me at Job's unswerving faith in the middle of losing everything he had physically.

While his body was wracked with pain. While he was in a situation any of us would clearly call hopeless.

After Job lost everything but praised God for it, he ended up losing his health. And then he was truly miserable. Scripture tells us he suffered sores and boils all over his body. It was then that his friends came and offered their ignorant observations and unsolicited conclusions about why Job was suffering. Scripture tells us Job was a righteous man, yet his friends questioned his righteousness, assuming he had some pride he wasn't aware of or a secret sin he was hiding from God and others. They were wrong in their assumptions. They had no idea what was going on in the heavenly realm—that Satan had challenged Job's faith and accused him of praising God only because God had given him everything. When Satan slandered Job before God, saying Job would curse God's name if God were to lift His hedge of protection around him and give Satan permission to inflict physical pain upon Job's body, the bet was on. God knew His faithful servant, Job. God was already preparing the reward for His servant's faithfulness. But Job had no idea all of that was happening in the heavenly realm. Job only knew that he was hurting, and God felt very far away.

Yet Job astounds us with another proclamation of his unswerving trust in God.

"Though He slay me, I will hope in Him."

Are you sensing the jaw-dropping silence from Job's friends?

Surprisingly, Job's statement wasn't . . .

"If You heal me, I'll continue to serve You."

"If You take away this pain, I'll sacrifice even more for You."

"If You restore all I have, I will live an even more righteous life."

"If You reverse all this, I'll write a book about it and go on the speaking circuit."

There was no bargaining in Job's statement. Just as he said after his first round of loss—"Naked I came from my mother's womb, and naked I will depart. The LORD gave and the LORD has taken away; may the name of the LORD be praised" (1:21 NIV)—his proclamation after his physical suffering was just as solid, perhaps even more so: "Though He slay me, I will hope in Him."

I recently became sick for the first time in several years. Even though it was "just a head cold" according to my husband, I literally thought I was going to die. During those four days of what I believed was sheer misery (I'm embarrassed about that now), my prayer was not "Though You slay me, I will hope in You." It was "Please help me recover quickly so I can write again." It was a deal, of sorts. "Do this for me, God, so I can do that for You."

Job was able to proclaim his hope in God because his hope didn't lie in his circumstances. Rather, it was cemented in his Creator. He wasn't hoping *for something*. He was hoping *in Someone*.

In Psalm 39, the songwriter eloquently expressed his hope *in God*, not for God to do something for him:

> LORD, remind me how brief my time on earth will be.
> > Remind me that my days are numbered—
> > how fleeting my life is.
> You have made my life no longer than the width of my hand.
> > My entire lifetime is just a moment to you;
> > at best, each of us is but a breath.
>
>
> We are merely moving shadows,
> > and all our busy rushing ends in nothing.

We heap up wealth,
    not knowing who will spend it.
And so, Lord, where do I put my hope?
    My *only hope* is in you (verses 4-7 NLT).

Not only was the psalmist's hope in God, but his *only hope* was in God. Not in God plus his family. Not in God plus his abilities, position, or influence. Not in God plus his financial security or savvy. His hope was in God *only*.

Hope is fragile. In fact, it's priceless. So don't just set it anywhere. Put it where's it's safe—in God.

Lord, help me to realize hope exists because You exist. You don't merely provide hope. You are hope. May my hope lie not in what You might do, but solely in Who You are.

TODAY'S CHALLENGE

Tell God your hope is in Him, regardless of what He does or doesn't do today.

DURING THE WAIT

The LORD is good to those who await Him,
to the person who seeks Him.

LAMENTATIONS 3:25

I t can feel so discouraging when you and I are praying for something and God doesn't appear to be answering.

Why are others enjoying the warmth of God's blessings while I'm being left out in the cold?, we wonder.

We scroll through social media and see one person after another reporting their #blessings and wonder why God is waiting when it comes to what *we* are hoping for. God's silence, or even a very clear *no* to our prayers, can add to our discouragement and leave us in a place where we are vulnerable to Satan's attacks on our faith and internal questions about whether God really cares about us.

Because the enemy's shouts of accusation can overpower the still, small voice of your loving Heavenly Father, you and I must know what to do—and what not to do—when God doesn't give us what we requested.

First, ***reacquaint yourself with God's truth.*** When you're feeling discouraged or abandoned by God due to unanswered prayer, that's often when Satan swoops in to launch his ruthless attack and give you thoughts that aren't your own. He will taunt you with lies like, "God stopped listening to you long ago." He will try to heap shame on you with accusations like, "Do you really think God will give you anything you ask for after what you've done?"

Counter the enemy's lies by familiarizing yourself with God's truth from His Word:

- He is merciful and compassionate (Lamentations 3:22-23).
- He is "righteous in all His ways, and kind in all His works" (Psalm 145:17).
- He is near to all who call on Him (Psalm 145:18).

When you know God is good and forgiving, and knows how to give good gifts to His children (Matthew 7:11), it will help you discern truth from falsehood and keep you from being easy prey to Satan's attacks during difficult times.

Second, ***remain faithful.*** Even though you might not feel you have what you want right now, remember that God so freely and generously gave you His Son. Romans 8:32 assures us, "He who did not spare his own Son but gave him up for us all, how will he not also with him graciously give us all things?" (ESV). Do you want to show an attitude of entitlement to that kind of generous and loving God? Or worse yet, resentment when you don't get what you want? God wants a *relationship* with you more than He wants your list of requests. He wants you to be satisfied in *Him*, not just what you receive from Him.

Jesus told a parable in Luke 18:1-8 of a widow who got what she wanted from an unrighteous judge simply because she wouldn't stop asking. Then Jesus pointed out how much more our loving Heavenly Father, who *is* righteous, will give justice to those who continually plead with Him their case. Remain faithful. Don't stop praying. Seek *Him*, instead of what you *want* from Him. It might make all the difference in what you're asking for, and you might even find you already have— in Him—all you could ever want.

Third, this is the time to ***record your blessings*** and what God has *already* granted. Start keeping track of what you do have. Writing down your prayer requests, as well as God's continued blessings—even the ones you don't ask for—can help you keep perspective. Record the date that He answers, whether it's a *yes* or *no*. You'll soon look back and see He *is* answering, and His *yes* responses may be more frequent than you realize. And His *no, not yet,* or *not in this way* responses may be more of a blessing than you realize.

Finally, ***redirect your requests*** to what He wants you to pray for. Have you ever asked God how to pray? "Lord, what should I pray for?" "Lord, how do *You* want me to pray?" "Lord, lay on my heart *Your* desires and make them mine."

When you and I pray according to God's lead, rather than expecting God to react and respond to our requests, it will completely change how we view and approach prayer altogether. We will discover there is *so much* He is doing in and around us, and *so much* He wants us to pray for so He can accomplish *so much more* than we ever thought possible.

Open my eyes, Lord Jesus, to what You want to accomplish in and around me, not to just what I want You to do. Help me to focus on the truth of Your Word, trust You to be faithful, recognize the answers You've already given me, and redirect my requests to reflect Your heart for me and others.

TODAY'S CHALLENGE

Ask God to lay upon your heart what He wants you to ask for. And thank Him, by faith, for the privilege of making your prayers a conduit through which He can perform His work here on Earth.

ALREADY AN OVERCOMER

You are from God, little children,
and have overcome them;
because greater is He who is in you
than he who is in the world.

1 JOHN 4:4

o you ever feel like it's an uphill struggle just to get through the day?

Perhaps you feel it's you against the world when it comes to your beliefs, values, or personal convictions.

Or maybe you're struggling with a person or circumstance that tends to bring out the worst in you.

It might seem that more and more, you are walking through your day with your head down in defeat. Life hurts. Disappointments abound. The struggle is real. Just being real.

But when you know God, and have His regenerating Holy Spirit dwelling within you, you possess a victorious spirit, one that can overcome.

In John 16:33, Jesus told His followers: "In the world you have tribulation, but take courage; I have overcome the world."

He has *overcome* the world. And He can help you overcome anything you struggle with in this world as well.

Oh, to be an overcomer.

My dad is an overcomer. He recently celebrated his fortieth sobriety birthday. Now in his late 80s, he is truly one who has overcome. He is active in his local Overcomers group—a Christ-based ministry for recovering addicts—and continues to be a sponsor (mentor) to other recovering alcoholics. Several days a week he is in a men's Bible study, participating in a prayer group or an Alanon or Overcomers support group, or attending Celebrate Recovery. What he loves the most is meeting personally with someone to encourage them in their recovery or their walk with Christ.

Most recovering alcoholics prefer the term *recovering* rather than *recovered*, lest pride cause them to fall back into their addiction. Yet Scripture tells us that in Christ, we are not *overcoming*—we have *already* overcome.

But overcome what?

Through Christ's life in you, you have overcome:

- the inevitability of death and eternal separation from God (Romans 6:22-23)
- the bondage of a life in which you were enslaved to sin (Romans 6:6)
- the inability to say no to temptation (1 Corinthians 10:13)
- a life ruled by the desires of your flesh (Romans 8:1-2, 9)

In Galatians 2:20, the apostle Paul gave us the key to living the life of an overcomer:

I have been crucified with Christ; and it is no longer I who live, but Christ lives in me; and the life which I now live in the flesh I live by faith in the Son of God, who loved me and gave Himself up for me.

When you live by faith in the power of Christ's resurrected life, and not in your own strength, you can overcome:

- the fear of death
- a state of hopelessness
- confusion over who you are
- your old way of thinking
- your former way of living
- a constant need for affirmation or purpose
- a driving desire for success as the world defines it
- doubts that you are loved

The next time you feel outnumbered, remember you're an overcomer through Christ.

The next time you feel outvoted, remember you're an overcomer, chosen by His grace.

The next time you feel outdated in your core values, beliefs, and convictions, remember you're an overcomer and one whom Jesus says is no longer part of this world (John 15:19).

The next time you feel ousted, remember you're an overcomer and will never be left out of what eternally matters. "How great a love the Father has given us, that we would be called children of God" (1 John 3:1).

What then shall we say to these things? If God is for us, who is against us? He who did not spare His own Son, but delivered Him over for us all, how will He not also with Him freely give us all things? Who will bring charges against [you]? God is the one who justifies; who is the one who condemns? Christ Jesus is He who died, but rather, was raised, who is at the right hand of God, who also intercedes for us. Who will separate us from the love of Christ? Will tribulation, or trouble, or persecution, or famine, or nakedness, or danger, or sword? (Romans 8:31-35).

No. "In all these things we overwhelmingly conquer through Him who loved us" (Romans 8:37).

Will you praise the Lord today for the power of His resurrection in you and the fact that you are, because of Him, more than a conqueror?

Thank You, Lord Jesus, that You have overcome the grave and through Your power, I can overcome even more. When I feel defeated, remind me that I am more than a conqueror through You.

TODAY'S CHALLENGE

Throughout the day, keep a list of all you have overcome with God's help. It may include unhealthy thoughts or habits, destructive behaviors, sins that used to entice you, or negative feelings toward others. Thank God for His strength with each victory you recall.

A HUNGER FOR MORE

*Blessed are those who hunger and
thirst for righteousness,
for they will be satisfied.*

MATTHEW 5:6

What are you hungry for today?

Peace? Joy? Recognition? Rest? Affirmation of the direction you've chosen? A more fulfilling relationship? An answer to a specific prayer request? A much-needed move in the direction of your purpose?

There is much to hunger for in this world. As humans, we specialize in hungering for what we can't have and still finding ourselves needing more.

Mick Jagger wasn't the first to sing about not being able to get any satisfaction.

Long before the Rolling Stones, King Solomon wrote a song expressing that sentiment:

No matter how much we see, we are never satisfied.
No matter how much we hear, we are not content
(Ecclesiastes 1:8 NLT).

Solomon, who had bought, tried, built, and experienced it all, spent
most of his song talking about the meaninglessness of life and its pur-
suits. But he concluded his song with this ageless gem: "Everything you
were taught can be put into a few words: Respect and obey God! This is
what life is all about" (Ecclesiastes 12:13 CEV).

Solomon affirmed to us that nothing in this world satisfies. And
that's why our hunger remains. The kind of hunger that can never be
satisfied, that is.

The sons of Korah wrote a song of hungering for God and expressed
a longing—a desperation—to be near Him:

> As the deer pants for the water brooks,
> so my soul pants for You, God.
> My soul thirsts for God, for the living God;
> when shall I come and appear before God?
> (Psalm 42:1-2).

That song was written in a time of trouble and exile and expressed
a desperation for God's protection and deliverance.

But what about longing for God simply because of Who He is, and
not because of how much we need Him for a certain problem or ongoing pain?

From the time I was young, I remember hearing others' salvation
stories. The pits they were trapped in, the depths of sin to which they
had sunk, the points of desperation they hit, and then the recognition
of their need for God. I remember praying, *God, I don't want to have to*

go through something really awful in order to be desperate for You. I want to be desperate for You now, even while life is good.

That desire, expressed by a ten-year-old Sunday school girl, wasn't so much a desire to avoid pain as it was a desire for God to know that I didn't need to experience the worst of the worst in order to long for Him.

My pain did come—through my parents' divorce and the breakup of our home at a time when I was transitioning from a teen to an adult and needed a solid foundation. Although my parents' divorce wasn't the catalyst for my trust in God, it deepened my conviction of His presence and His love and helped me cling to Him tighter. And at a time when I believed I had lost everything else, I realized He was all I had.

Today I still sense a hunger, at times, for other things. But when it strikes, I remind myself that when I have God, I have all I will ever need. The days when I feel alone, I am not. The aloneness comes from listening to my feelings rather than the facts of His Word, which says, "I will never leave you nor forsake you" (Hebrews 13:5). The days I feel weak, it's because I have forgotten the power of Christ that dwells in me. The days I feel I am losing something (people, relationships, trust, respect, significance, youth, vitality, influence) are the days I must remember that He is my greatest possession.

Are you hungry for more joy? Come into His presence with joyful singing (Psalm 100:2) because Scripture tells us joy exists in His presence (Psalm 16:11).

Are you hungry for significance? God's first recorded breath on this earth gave life to man (Genesis 2:7), and He gave up His last breath on Earth, prior to His resurrection, to save him (Matthew 27:50). That tells us how significant we are to Him. It also reminds us that our very life and salvation is dependent upon the breath of God.

Are you hungry for purpose? God says we were created in Christ Jesus for good works that God prepared beforehand that we should walk in them (Ephesians 2:10).

Are you hungry for personal and spiritual growth? Get into God's Word and you'll be like a tree planted by a stream whose leaves don't wither in the desert heat and that survives the drought of troubling times (Psalm 1:2-3; Jeremiah 17:7-8).

Are you hungry for satisfaction or pleasure? Psalm 34:8 tells us to "taste and see that the LORD is good." Taste of His goodness, His love, His justice, His ways.

There is much we can be desperate for today. Fleeting things. Things that will never satisfy. But there is only one who satisfies and will never disappoint. Be hungry for Him. Be *desperate* for Him. And He promises in Jeremiah 29:13, "You will seek Me *and find Me* when you search for Me with all your heart."

Lord, make me desperate for You today...You alone. May the "more" I desire simply be more of You.

TODAY'S CHALLENGE

Make a list of all that you have because you have Christ Jesus. This list can be of tangible things as well as intangible. It can also be ongoing in a journal or on your device. Add to it every time you think of something else.

DESPERATE FOR HIS TOUCH

*A woman who had been suffering from a hemorrhage
for twelve years came up behind Him, and
touched the border of His cloak; for she was saying to
herself, "If I only touch His cloak, I will get well."*

MATTHEW 9:20-21

Scripture tells us of a woman who was so desperate for God's healing and transforming power in her life that she was willing to risk ridicule and possibly even punishment just to *touch* Jesus. We don't know her name, nor where she was from. We only know her condition: She had been bleeding for *12 years.* Under Jewish law, her hemorrhaging made her ritually unclean and therefore, a social outcast. She couldn't touch—or be touched—by anyone or they would be considered unclean as well. What a lonely, isolated, affection-starved existence she must've lived. Broken as a person, emotionally and physically, she was also broken financially, having spent everything she had trying to find a cure. At her wits' end—physically, emotionally, and financially—she went looking for Jesus.

We tend to do that, don't we? When we're finally at our wits' end—relationally, emotionally, physically, or financially—we seek out a miracle touch from Jesus.

This woman must have realized the scorn or punishment she would receive for touching Jesus. But in spite of her fear, she took the risk. She worked her way through the crowd and managed to touch the edge of Jesus' clothing. Her *faith*, which resulted in her desperation to touch the only one who could heal her, made her whole and complete.

Can you relate to wanting Jesus' touch so badly that you're willing to do *anything* to get it? Perhaps not. If we are honest with ourselves, most of us, myself included, will admit that we would long for His touch more if we thought we really needed it. If we were physically ill. Or if we were financially desperate. Or if we were emotionally broken. But you and I need His touch any time we've grown complacent in our faith or forgotten how intimately acquainted He is with our lives and how much He wants us depending on Him for everything, including the very air we breathe.

I recently experienced a health scare that had me praying, once again, for God's touch.

Please touch this mass in my body and eliminate any sign of cancer. Please touch my emotions and calm my fears in the midst of all the what ifs. Please touch my heart and mind so my response to the diagnosis—whatever it is—will be pleasing to You.

I hadn't realized God had *already* touched me with that mass and the uncertainty surrounding it so I could see a precious new side of His love and be reacquainted with how intimately familiar He is with all my ways. Experiencing God's touch of comfort and His attention to the tiniest details of my life during that time made me wonder how

I had ever existed without a daily awareness of His presence and work on my behalf. I realize now He was preparing me for the most heart-wrenching week of my life—five months later—when I would hold my mom's hand and stroke her head and assure her of God's touch on *her* life as He gently carried her home.

When suffering or uncertainty strikes—whether it be a sudden injury or illness that has you bedridden, or a heartache or loss that causes your insides to feel as if they are being ripped to shreds—you have an opportunity to be desperate for the One whose touch heals. You have a chance to gain a greater awareness of His presence and experience the God of heaven reaching down and touching your heart and circumstances. And you get to be another glory story of His healing touch.

> If Job could have known as he sat there in the ashes, bruising his heart on this problem of providence—that in the trouble that had come upon him he was doing what one man may do to work out the problem for the world, he might again have taken courage. No man lives to himself. Job's life is but your life and mine written in larger text…So then, though we may not know what trials wait on any of us, we can believe that, as the days in which Job wrestled with his dark maladies are the only days that make him worth remembrance, and but for which his name had never been written in the Book of Life, so the days through which we struggle, finding no way, but never losing the light, will be the most significant we are called to live.[7]

Lord, thank You for the ways You have touched my life and made me desperate for You because my spiritual health is far more important than my temporary fears or struggles.

TODAY'S CHALLENGE

What ongoing issues in your life cause you to need God's healing touch? Or what issues have you lived with for so long that you've resigned yourself to ever being healed or completely freed? Talk with Him about those issues now as you realize your pain is often connected to your purpose.

GIVING HIM YOUR STRESS

*Consider the lilies, how they grow: they
neither labor nor spin;
but I tell you, not even Solomon in all his
glory clothed himself like one of these.*

Luke 12:27

I recently heard that 90 percent of young moms today feel stressed. Do you know one? Maybe you *are* one.

Alexa, a mom of two children under age three, says she constantly feels she should be doing more every day, like cleaning, spending time with God, cultivating friendships, taking care of her health, and more. And the more she does without slowing down to care for her soul, the more stressed she feels.

"When I don't take the time to emotionally unpack things and instead shove them down, the emotions continue to bubble up and cause me to feel overwhelmed.

"Sometimes I feel as if God is far away; other times I feel like He's near. In the beginning of a new struggle, it's easy to feel alone and that

God is not in the situation with me. But as I try to control my emotions more, I'm able to remind myself of the truths about God: He's sovereign over all, He cares more about me than the birds in the air and the flowers in the field, and He will never leave me nor forsake me."

Alexa has grabbed hold of a foundational truth: God cares for His children, so why do we worry?

No matter our age, we tend to forget that we are of utmost importance to our Creator, Sustainer, and Redeemer. God speaks so tenderly of the birds and then tells us how much more we mean to Him than these creatures of flight.

Yet circumstances still arise, at times, that cause us to wonder, even if only for a moment, whether God is still in control.

How could this happen?

Why would God allow this at the worst possible time?

Doesn't God realize I can't handle one thing more?

Yet Alexa, who has learned to trust God during the stressful times, realizes sanctification—a holiness and growth and purity that sets us apart for His purposes—takes time.

"It all comes down to the slow process of sanctification," she said. "I want to pray to God for a change and see it happen instantly—or in my timing instead of His. But just like when planting a fruit tree, it takes time and intentionality to cultivate the fruit of the Spirit. And it's all God's doing. Not my own."

Are you looking to the Lord to slowly grow you, refine you, draw you closer to Himself, and produce more of His character (the fruit of the Spirit) in you?

Galatians 5:22-23 tells us "the fruit of the Spirit is love, joy, peace, patience, kindness, goodness, faithfulness, gentleness, self-control; against such things there is no law."

Are you letting God grow these characteristics within you, which will help you get through anything? Are you letting Him comfort you and remind you that you are not alone? Are you letting Him strengthen you through whatever comes your way?

If not, it might be time to surrender everything to Him and truly believe He wants to help. "Believe God's Word and power more than you believe your own feelings and experiences. Your Rock is Christ, and it is not the Rock which ebbs and flows, but your seas."[8]

Isaiah 30:15 says, "In quietness and trust is your strength." In the New Century Version, that verse reads, "If you will be calm and trust me, you will be strong."

Alexa wisely recognizes that her mental and emotional state is often a direct result of the amount of time she spends with God and the truths of His Word, which can help balance her emotions and remind her of Who is ultimately in control of all things.

"I need to stop making excuses for why I'm too busy to spend time with Him," she admits. "I have the time. I just prefer to spend it doing something else. But when I spend consistent time with Him, He reveals Himself profoundly and in beautiful ways."

There is something beautiful that the Maker of your soul wants to reveal to you in the midst of your busyness, your disappointments, and your concerns. There is a satisfaction in Him alone that He wants you to discover—or remember—during your stress. There is a peace and calm found only in Him that He wants you to experience regardless of what is swirling around you.

Can you give Him your stress today, realizing He loves you more than anything and He's waiting to carry these concerns for you?

> *Lord, how I long to be calm and trust You and there find my strength. Thank You that You care for me more than I realize. Help me to quiet my heart and trust in Your care.*

TODAY'S CHALLENGE

What is the most pressing issue or task on your mind today? Commit it to God and trust that He will clear the way for you to get it done if that's truly necessary.

CALMING YOUR HEART WITH WORSHIP

Commit everything you do to the LORD.
Trust him, and he will help you.

PSALM 37:5 NLT

*A*re you feeling overwhelmed today with too much to accomplish in too little time? Maybe you're feeling a bit of guilt, too, in the midst of your busy schedule, for not taking adequate time to be with God daily. Or perhaps you simply feel the world—or *your* world—is an out-of-control mess.

Then worship Him, my friend. Just worship.

Worship feeds our soul and reminds us of our purpose, which is to glorify God in all we do. If you are lacking spiritual energy and focus and feeling complacency set in, that's your spirit telling you to put it all aside for a moment and focus on God's worth-ship. Just like the human body needs food, water, movement, and sleep to maintain health and vigor, your soul needs to worship its Creator to be refreshed, refueled, and reenergized.

Worship keeps us focused on God, not ourselves. We can so easily be all about ourselves and all we have to *do.* Our self-love mentality can make us believe we exist for ourselves. Yet we exist to glorify God. Focusing on God's worth-ship moves us out of the picture and lets Him take the spotlight. John the Baptist said this about Jesus: "He must increase, but I must decrease" (John 3:30). That's what worship does; it magnifies God and shrinks us, as it should be. In *The Message*, that verse reads: "This is the assigned moment for [Jesus] to move into the center, while I slip off to the sidelines." Worship puts the spotlight on God and places us back in the humble position of seeing our need to grow spiritually.

Worship is a witness to the world of whom we love. We all worship—or serve—something: our lifestyles, our diets, our homes, our workout goals or our bodies, our careers, our viewpoints, our relationships. Sometimes we worship money or fame, possessions or people, social status, substances, or self. Jesus said, "You cannot serve God *and* wealth" (Matthew 6:24). Because the desire to worship is ingrained in us, and we all worship *something*, taking the time to admire God's magnificence in all He has created reminds us that He—not possessions, fame, social status, substances, nor any created thing—is worthy of our adoration and devotion. He alone is our greatest possession, worthy of all our worship. King David, who was described by God as "a man after My heart" (Acts 13:22), sang, "LORD, you *alone* are my portion and my cup" (Psalm 16:5 NIV).

I recently saw a slogan that read, "#SelfLove is my new relationship status." That may sound good on the surface, but it represents how far we have fallen in our understanding of who we are and what we were made to worship. Our number one relationship must be with God, or you and I won't know how to love anyone else, including ourselves. While God sees us as valued and cherished, it is only through His Son's redemption of us that our value exists. Without Jesus, we are lost in our sins, even though we're loved. Yet when we accept His offer of salvation by trusting in His atoning death for us on Calvary, God sees us as just as valuable as His own Son, who redeemed us. Our love is to be first for Him, then for others. We are to respect ourselves as made in the image of God, and value our hearts, minds, and bodies as the temple of God, but there is a huge difference between self-care and self-love, between self-respect and self-worship.

Jesus told us to deny ourselves (our fleshly instincts and our sense of entitlement), and consider ourselves crucified—as He was—so His risen self can live through us (Galatians 2:20). When He lives through us, His preferences, His character, His righteousness, His attributes become ours. When I consider all that He gave up for me, there is no question whom the object of my worship should be.

Do you need suggestions for some practical ways to put yourself aside and worship your Maker, Creator, Sustainer, and Savior? Here are a few:

- Go outside and verbally praise God for everything you see.

- Open your Bible to the Psalms and sing them (yes, sing!). They are all songs originally set to music. Make up a tune or sing to a melody you already know.

- Praise God through the ABCs by naming a characteristic of God's that starts with every letter of the alphabet and praising Him for it. (For example, "God, You are *awesome* and *able.* Lord, You are *beautiful!* I thank You for being *creative, caring,* and *comforting.* I praise You for being my *defender* and a *delight* to my soul…)

- Play some instrumental or praise and worship music and reflect on the majesty of God.

As you reflect on God's worth-ship, He will draw you closer and calm your anxious heart. Every single time.

Lord, I recognize Your worth, majesty, goodness, and lovingkindness. Thank You for desiring my praise and for calming my heart as I focus it on You, the only one who can care for all that concerns me.

TODAY'S CHALLENGE

Look for ways to worship God, praise Him for Who He is, and thank Him for a few moments every hour on the hour.

ALL THAT MATTERS

Teach us to number our days,
that we may present to You a heart of wisdom.

Psalm 90:12

We all have to-do lists that can feel overwhelming at times. Whether you keep yours on paper like I still do, and relish the joy of crossing through each task, or your list exists in the notes section of your phone or inside your mind, we all feel that burdening sense of *all that I must do.*

Some of what's on that list is important. If you don't shop for groceries, what will you eat? If laundry isn't done, what will you wear? If the project isn't sectioned out in steps and worked on daily, when will it get completed? Yet what on that list will matter a year from now, ten years from now, or in view of eternity?

Somehow, somewhere, the almighty To-Do List rose up before women and called itself God. And we continue to bow down to it.

Having been raised with a strong work ethic (or maybe it's my type-A driven personality I often wish I didn't have), I used to find it difficult to be "unproductive," even when I was on vacation, or when I was feeling worn down and my body was saying, "Rest!" I used to find it more difficult to slow down and not get things done than to muster up the motivation to do them. Yet the older I get, the more joy I am experiencing when I put aside the to-do list and prioritize people over productivity.

In Psalm 90:12, Moses asked God to help him realize his days were numbered so he could live wisely. In a modern translation that verse reads, "Oh! Teach us to live well! Teach us to live wisely and well!" (MSG). What if you and I were to number our *days* instead of our tasks? What if we were to make a list of what we wanted to do wisely and well each day (and before we die), rather than focus on all the meaningless tasks that seem to be setting our schedules and ruling our days and minds?

When I get to heaven one day, there will be no reward for the amount of money I made or how far up I advanced on the corporate ladder. There will be no accolades for the number of followers I had on social media, or the number of hits on my website, or the number of views on my YouTube videos. There won't be any kudos for having the loveliest seasonal decorations, or being the most organized member of the team, or accomplishing the most at the company. There is so much that we tend to honor or strive for or prioritize that doesn't mean anything to God in the scope of eternity.

In Micah 6:8, we are told what God honors:

> He has told you, mortal one, what is good;
> and what does the LORD require of you
> but to do justice, to love kindness,
> and to walk humbly with your God?

Wow, where is *that* on my to-do list? Where is it on yours?

To do justly, love kindness, and walk humbly with God amounts to tasks that benefit others. It involves serving. It involves assignments that might not be on the list at all, but rather, compete with our tasks and add to our frustrations at being inconvenienced or delayed. God works on a different timeline than we do, so that might be why He isn't sympathetic toward our rush, rush, rush. And it might be why He continues to convict our hearts to *slow down*.

God gave us enough hours in the day to do all that's needed to fulfill our purpose in Him (to love Him and others and glorify Him in all we do). The things on your list that may seem necessary to you might not be that important to Him, or to anyone else, for that matter. Sometimes we put more pressure on ourselves than we need to.

Yet as much as we'd like to walk away from our to-do list, we often let that blasted piece of paper, or that running list on our phones or in the back of our minds, dictate how much we will enjoy life, how much time we will spend in a call (a phone call, not a text) to a friend or family member, and how much time we will spend (not "waste") on tasks that don't look like accomplishment to the world, but represent wealth to the Lord.

O Lord, help me to focus on the few things that really matter. Help me bring balance to my to-do list by making sure that people-related activities or tasks are on there. Don't let me spend my life in paperwork, computer work, or busywork that won't amount to anything one day. As I number my lists, help me to number my days by making sure they are filled with purpose.

TODAY'S CHALLENGE

Focus on the tasks on your to-do list that will most benefit those you love.
Sometimes it's the simple acts of love that reap the most results eternally.

NOTHING BESIDES HIM

Whom have I in heaven but you?
And there is nothing on earth
that I desire besides you.

My flesh and my heart may fail,
but God is the strength of my heart
and my portion forever.

PSALM 73:25-26 ESV

Does it sometimes feel like the world is passing you by?

A friend posts of her romantic weekend in Cancun, and another one boasts of her promotion at her dream job.

You see happy family pictures and wonder if you'll ever be able to post one. And the new home video looks more like a palace tour. To top it off, a colleague tells you about a party she attended during the week, assuming you got an invite, and you didn't.

Everybody seems to be living the #blessed life, but what about you?

God understands those deep aches and longings in our hearts to belong, to succeed, to feel significant, happy, and fulfilled. What we might call FOMO ("fear of missing out"), He sees as that deep longing He allows us to have so He can draw us back toward Himself.

God's foremost desire for you is that you love Him with all your heart, soul, mind, and strength, and love and prefer others as much as you love and prefer your own self (Matthew 22:37-39). His will is that you and I be thankful and content in all things (1 Thessalonians 5:18), and seek Him—and obedience to Him—before anything else (Matthew 6:33).

"Whom have I in heaven but You?," Asaph sang in Psalm 73:25. "And besides You, I desire nothing on earth" (NASB 1995).

What would it take for you and me to be able to sing that, to really believe that, even at times when we feel we're missing out?

"My flesh and my heart may fail," the psalmist continued, "but God is the strength of my heart and my portion forever" (verse 26).

When Scripture says God is our "portion forever" it means we have our inheritance, our future, all we will ever need. And we have it in Him—in an obedient and surrendered life to Him. All the rest is icing on the cake as He chooses to bless us according to the deep desires of our hearts, and for our eternal well-being.

But what about those who aren't obedient to God and don't live a surrendered life to Him? They still seem to have all that they want—and many times what you and I want. Yet a realization of what they have, and what *we* have in Jesus, can help change our perspective and align our attitude.

The songwriter concludes his song with this truth: "Those who are far from You will perish…But as for me, the nearness of God is good for me" (verses 27-28).

God knows every detail of your life. As you surrender it to Him and seek His best for you, He will guide you toward a life of joy. Your life won't look exactly like everyone else's or even *anyone* else's. But the Maker of your soul knows how to fulfill *your* heart. And He longs for you to arrive at the place where you can joyfully say, "The nearness of God is good for me."

How many women post on social media about how much they have of the *nearness of God*? How many brag that they've found their greatest possession in Him? The "nearness of God" is not just something we have on days we can emotionally feel it. The "nearness of God" is a promise of His when He says, "I will never leave you nor forsake you" (Hebrews 13:5 ESV). This isn't something that comes and goes depending on your circumstances or how you feel. It is a constant. A fact. A solid truth upon which you can build your life.

There have been four heartbreaking seasons in my life, when I had to remind myself that Jesus was all I had and all I wanted: the day my parents' marriage collapsed, the day I lost the man I thought I would marry, the day I thought I would lose my daughter, and the day I saw my mother leave this earth. Knowing on every one of those days that Jesus was still there and would never leave changed *everything*.

Can you tell Jesus today, "In heaven I have only you, and on this earth you are all I want"? (Psalm 73:25 CEV). You might not feel it at the time, but God has a way of changing your heart to align with His when you obediently seek Him above all things. As you speak these words, God will make this the desire of your heart.

Lord Jesus, whom do I have but You? You are all I want. No matter what life looks like for everyone else, I will maintain that You are my joy, my portion, and my reward. Give me a heart that lives this so I can experience Your joy. And may I be able to honestly say Your nearness, the closeness we share, is the very best I can hope for—and have—in all of this life.

TODAY'S CHALLENGE

Reflect on what this world has to offer and how it pales in comparison to knowing Jesus and having His nearness. Then think about all that awaits you in His presence.

ALL THAT YOU NEED

You, Lord, are all I want!
You are my choice,
and you keep me safe.
You make my life pleasant,
and my future is bright.

Psalm 16:5-6 CEV

How easy it must have been for David, the psalmist, to say, "You, Lord, are all I want!" After all, he was the anointed king of Israel with several wives, several children, and a kingdom that adored him.

Perhaps if you and I possessed *half* of what David did, or even half of what we *wanted*, we'd be able to express the fulfillment he did.

Yet it is ingrained into the fabric of our nature as women to want to be with someone, help someone, and feel supported, encouraged, cherished, desired, and a valuable part of one's team. We want a sense of family, security and stability, purpose, and constant affirmation.

I have often wondered if *anyone* ever arrives at a place of total contentment, a place where they can say, "I have all I want."

"I have all I *need*" is a different story. Our needs are often very different from our wants. The word *need* implies necessity for sustenance and survival—food, shelter, purpose, hope. There is so much we want and often *think* we need: security, financial stability, a sense of identity and affirmation of who we are and what we are doing. Yet once we come to the place where we realize the Lord is all we *need*, we are getting closer to being able to say, as the psalmist did, "You, Lord, are all I *want*!"

God designed you and me to be completely fulfilled in Him. He promises in His Word to provide all we need. But He also promises to be the fulfiller of our desires.

David, the shepherd boy who became king, likely wrote Psalm 16 before he was admired and revered as Israel's greatest monarch. Because the song opens with his request for safety, it is believed he wrote it while he was in danger, possibly when he was running for his life from King Saul, who wanted him dead. David had many years during which he struggled, and he drew closer to his Lord in the midst of those struggles.

If David wrote this song *after* being promised Israel's throne—but still not receiving it for several more years—he was declaring, by faith, regardless of his present circumstances, that God's future for him was bright. Can you and I say, even when circumstances aren't perfect (or even *close* to being perfect), "You, Lord, are all I want"?

You and I likely don't have a dynasty in our future. But we have the same God who lifted up a shepherd boy who was content with God alone, and who made him Israel's most loved and respected king. David once prayed, "My soul, wait in silence for God alone, for my hope is from Him" (Psalm 62:5). As you and I wait on God and His timing, we will not be disappointed.

Yet sometimes we expect our hopes to be realized before we're willing to declare something by faith.

Once I'm engaged to be married, I will be convinced my future is bright.

Once I'm able to have a child, I'll know my life is turning out as I want.

Once I secure that career (or coveted position in the company), I'll be able to say, "God's plan for me is good."

But that's not faith. Scripture tells us to walk by faith, not by sight (2 Corinthians 5:7). Walk according to what and in Whom you believe, not according to what you can see.

Even if you don't have all that you want today, even if you don't see your future secured, can you exercise faith that because God said it, it is so? Can you see it with your eyes because He has already seen it and assured you of its reality? Just as surely as you're hoping in heaven, can you keep your hope fixed on the ultimate Promise Keeper, who promises to give you the happily ever after in the best way possible for you in this life and beyond?

Can you say it now—"You, Lord, are all I want! You are my choice, and you keep me safe. You make my life pleasant, and my future is bright"? Can you say this simply because He has already declared it for those who love Him, and you trust Him to keep His Word?

Trust God today, regardless of what you see or don't see ahead of you. As He becomes all you want, you will soon discover you have all you will ever need.

Lord, I believe the psalmist's words that You keep me safe and my future is bright. Help me to be content in You alone so I can say, as David did, "You, LORD, are all I want!"

TODAY'S CHALLENGE

Tell God why He is all you want and make it the prayer of your heart throughout the day. As you do, you will be growing one step closer to His purpose for you—to love Him and enjoy Him forever.

YOUR EVER AFTER

You will make known to me the way of life;
in Your presence is fullness of joy;
in Your right hand there are pleasures forever.

PSALM 16:11

I f you ever feel like the odd one out, the different one, the overlooked one, you are not alone.

It can be especially easy these days to feel alone as a lover of Jesus and one who stands apart from the world. Even family members may not believe as you do. What you know to be true is slammed in the media and questioned in the schools.

Will we ever feel like we belong in this culture? Not likely. But persevering gets easier when we long for heaven.

You have One who has gone before you, Who has paved the path for you, and Who promises that one day you'll be at home with Him.

Yet we sometimes believe we need to *see* God at work—experience the miracles, see the evidence, recognize the divine appointments—to be assured of His presence. Why do we constantly seek affirmation that He is with us, still working in our lives, still sovereign over the chaos of this world?

He has given you and me every indication of His presence by His transforming power in our lives—whenever we do something indicative of the redeemed, and every time we see another life and heart that He has changed.

And the people He brings into your life to show you Christ's love, to be Jesus' serving hands, to offer God's gentle wisdom—they are evidence of His presence too.

After talking with several women recently, all in their late 20s and early 30s, it was remarkable to me how many times they mentioned the need for community, for someone to talk with, and share openly and honestly. Some didn't have a local church or feel they could find that honesty there. Others had full schedules and couldn't foresee having the time it takes to develop close friendships. Then, in talking with women in their 40s and 50s, they said the same thing. "When I'm doing life with others, openly and honestly, sharing my struggles and putting myself in a position where I can glean wisdom from other women, I feel far more supported and much less alone," one middle-aged woman told me.

When we live among like-minded believers, we feel much less alone.

You and I were not meant to be isolated Jesus-followers, lone-ranger Christians, women who walk alone. We were made for intimacy with God and genuine, honest community with one another. As you grow closer to God and share with others what you are learning, true friendships will forge, genuine trust will develop, Christian community will happen. But sometimes you have to initiate it. Seek out others whom you can encourage toward a closer relationship with Jesus, and you'll find God brings to you exactly whom you need for your own growth, support, and joy.

Earlier, we looked at David's beautiful proclamation from Psalm 16:5-6: "You, LORD, are all I want! You are my choice, and you keep me safe" (CEV). He said this when he didn't necessarily have all that he wanted at that point in his life. Then we looked at the next line of David's song and how he could possibly proclaim his bright future while he was likely under attack.

While living on the run without a roof over his head or solid ground under his feet, while a refugee, while undoubtedly stressed, David was still assured of God's presence. More than that, he *knew* beyond a doubt that his future was bright.

David, this man who was assured of God's constant presence, knew that from beginning to end, God is faithful. God is the ultimate Promise Keeper, the ever-capable Provider, the never-misses-a-thing Protector. He is the One who has written your story before you, and He can get you safely to the end chapter, the happily ever after, the bright future He has in store for you.

Trust Him now. And you will see your future—with Him at your side—unfolding before your eyes. When David proclaimed in Psalm 16 that God alone was his portion and his cup, that his lot was secure, that the boundary lines had fallen in pleasant places for him, and that his heritage was beautiful to him (verses 5-6), he saw what you and I can see when we trust the Promise Keeper to carry us safely over the threshold into our eternal home.

The rest of Psalm 16 not only tells us our heavenly reward is awaiting us, but celebrates what we can experience through intimate closeness with Jesus while we're still here on this earth. David ends his song with a praise to God—a praise we can echo because He is at our side:

> You make known to me the path of life; you will fill me with joy in your presence, with eternal pleasures at your right hand (verse 11 NIV).

Thank You, Lord Jesus, that a bright future truly awaits me because, in You, there is fullness of joy and I never ever walk alone.

YOUR CHALLENGE FROM THIS DAY FORWARD

Continue to look to the One who holds your future in His right hand and declares it bright. He knows exactly how to get you to your happily ever after with Him.

A CLOSING WORD FROM CINDI

Thank you so much for reading *The New Loneliness Devotional*. I'm glad we've had this time together to draw closer to God's heart, and prayerfully closer to others God has surrounded us with. If you haven't yet read my full-length book *The New Loneliness*, it will help you go further in nurturing meaningful relationships with God and others so you don't feel so isolated.

Please visit my website at www.StrengthForTheSoul.com and leave me a note letting me know you were there. You can share how you've been encouraged by this book, find out more about my speaking ministry and other books, and sign up for my encouraging emails so we can keep in touch.

I hope to hear from you soon!

Cindi

SCRIPTURE VERSIONS
USED IN THIS BOOK

NOTES

1. The full report from the US Surgeon General can be found here: https://www.hhs.gov
   /about/news/2023/05/03/new-surgeon-general-advisory-raises-alarm-about
   -devastating-impact-epidemic-loneliness-isolation-united-states.html.

2. These statistics are from 2021: https://www.cdc.gov/suicide/facts/index.html.

3. An article linking stress to cancer and other health issues can be found here: https://
   www.mdanderson.org/publications/focused-on-health/how-stress-affects-cancer-risk
   .h21-1589046.html.

4. Lloyd John Ogilvie, *God's Best for My Life* (Eugene, OR: Harvest House, 1981), 18.

5. Ogilvie, *God's Best for My Life*, 19.

6. For more on developing a more intimate relationship with God, see Cindi's book
   Letting God Meet Your Emotional Needs (Eugene, OR: Harvest House, 2000).

7. Robert Collyar, quoted in Mrs. Charles E. Cowman, *Streams in the Desert* (Grand
   Rapids, MI: Zondervan, 1965), 169.

8. Samuel Rutherford, quoted in Mrs. Charles E. Cowman, *Streams in the Desert* (Grand
   Rapids, MI: Zondervan, 1965), 87.

OTHER BOOKS BY CINDI MCMENAMIN

 *The New Loneliness*—Exploring how our current cultural environment and reliance on technology have hindered our ability to connect, Cindi McMenamin provides biblical insights and action steps for deepening your relationships with God and others.

When Women Walk Alone—Through the examples of biblical and contemporary women, you'll find practical, comforting steps for dealing with loneliness. Offers help in finding support from others, celebrating uniqueness, and gaining strength for single–parenting challenges.

 *When a Woman Overcomes Life's Hurts*—Explores the kinds of hurt women experience and offers gracious biblical counsel on how and where to find healing. This is a book filled with grace, redemption, and transformation.

When God Sees Your Tears—In times of heartache, you may wonder if God even cares. You've poured your heart out to Him, but when the answers don't seem to come, you wonder if He is listening. In this book you'll discover that yes, your tears are seen, your prayers are heard, and the comfort God offers is real.

 When Couples Walk Together—This 31-day devotional offers simple, helpful (and fun!) steps a husband and wife can take to nourish closeness and intimacy. Includes activities, prayers, and anecdotal tips.